megatokyo

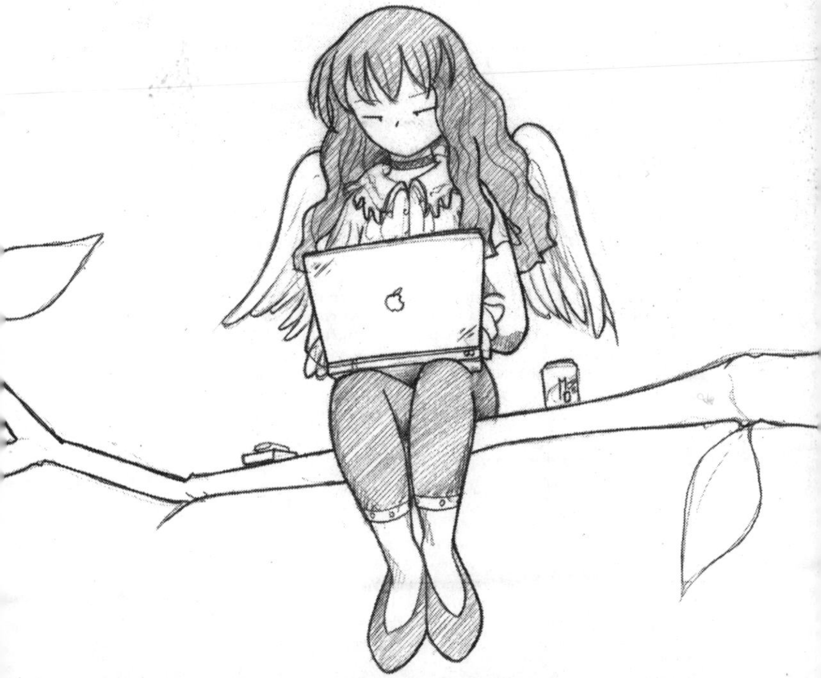

MEGATOKYO™ Volume 1

STORY & ART BY FRED GALLAGHER
Story & Co-Creation By Rodney Caston
Stick art by Dominic Nguyen

Type Placement and Layout by Ellen Ohlmacher
under the Art Direction of Fred Gallagher

Additional editing for Second Printing by Stephanie Brown

Megatokyo™ Graphic Novel Volume 1, December 2002.
© 2002 Fred Gallagher. Publication rights arranged between Fred Gallagher and I.C. Entertainment.
All rights reserved. Nothing from this book may be reproduced without written consent from
the copyright holder(s). Violators will be prosecuted to the full extent of the laws
of the United States of America. All persons and events in this production are fictitious.
Any similarity to actual persons or evens is unintentional.

Printed in the United States.

Second Printing

"Megatokyo" TM, U.S. registration pending,
is a trademark of Fredart Studios, LLC.

Published by I.C. Entertainment
1005 Mahone Street, Suite 102
Fredericksburg, VA 22401

Find this title and many more on our website
www.ic-ent.com

megatokyo

volume 1
"relax, we understand jOO"

story & art:
Fred Gallagher

story & co-creator:
Rodney Caston

stick figures:
Dominic Nguyen

www.megatokyo.com

published by
I.C. Entertainment
www.ic-ent.com

There is no way I can list all of the people who have inspired, supported,
encouraged and helped with Megatokyo over the past two years, but I'll try:

Rodney Caston (Largo)
Dominic Nguyen (Dom)
Edmund Balan (Ed)
Ken Hashimoto (Asmodeus)
Jon Montroll (Ukyo)
Keishi Tada (tsubasa)
Christi Heiskell (Natsuki)
August Kaiser (Kai)
Lisa Konopacki (Crowqueen)
Jerry Levine (Patchmonkey)
Kristen Perry (Merekat)
Richard Kim (Pocky)
Scott Crain (cortana)

Omoikane, Milkchan, Zen
Dillinger, Lem and Crow for
helping to keep the forums
under control.

Tenebrae (my goth advisor!)
Sogarth, AJ, Ping-chan, Wombat
NinjaStu, Suncrusher, Mike, J. Duddles
KimJustice (for all the great music)
SPOONprez, Ender, DevilBunny, S. Argenziano
K. Patterson, Bonzai, DJ Batz, Peter, Fred,
Seiya, Moeru, Kuromaku, Fuchikoma,
And the rest of the #f crew.
The #megatokyo regulars for
putting up with me.

Kei and Ellen for all
the hard work they put in
to help make this book
happen, thanks!

To Mom, Dad and
my sister, Jen, for
all their support.

And finally,
for Sarah
with love.

C O N T E N T S

<piro>
what is megatokyo?

I don't remember exactly when Rodney started to bug me about doing a webcomic.

He had been hosting my art website 'Fredart.com' for several months, and we spent a lot of time hanging out in the same IRC channels. Rod was a big fan of online comics and read quite a few of them regularly. At the time, I didn't really know much about webcomics. I was a hardcore old school anime/manga/game fan who spent most of his time browsing Japanese websites.

I got a lot of "Dude, you gotta read this! You could do this!" messages from Rod followed by URLs to various webcomic sites. It wasn't long before I found myself reading and enjoying sites like Penny Arcade, PVP Online, Sluggy Freelance, Exploitation Now, Sinfest and Real Life. Even though most of these were of the 'gag-a-day' genre, there was a lot of depth, hilarity, and creative energy that kept me coming back.

Even though I was now reading and enjoying these comics, I still felt no desire to actually make one. My art style was anime-manga inspired, and I wanted to do serious, multi-page, manga-style comics with complex stories, not single strip gags. There was also the fact that I had never done sequential work before. Most of my work at the time was stand alone character illustrations. The concept of drawing the same character twice, or even two characters in the same frame, was daunting.

One of the reasons I started Fredart many years ago was to put some of my sketches online and see how people reacted to them. For years I wanted to do a "doujinshi," which are small, self-published comics sold at conventions like Comike in Tokyo. While Rodney was trying to talk me into doing a webcomic, I was busy working on a short story called "Envelope." This project was an illustrated story my friend Tsubasa and I were working on for a doujinshi CD-rom collection. It was really my first attempt at sequential artwork, and in the end, it came out better than I expected (if you're curious, there are links to it on my website). The individual pieces of artwork sucked, but as a whole, it amazed me how effectively it told the story.

After "Envelope" was finished, I wanted to get back to working on my main project, a manga-style love story called "Warmth." I had spent several months developing the story and its characters, but I felt that I still didn't have the drawing skills necessary to pull it off. My success with "Envelope" encouraged me to give it another try.

I still wasn't sure how I was going to release "Warmth." I figured that I would self-publish and try to sell it at Comike, like any other doujinshi. Still, it seemed like a lot of work to fly all the way to Japan just to sell a few books. I considered releasing it directly to the web, but decided against it. Stories require a certain amount of emotive commitment from the people who read them. You can't just read one page of a book every other week and expect to enjoy it. You need to be able to sit down, get involved, and have a reasonable amount of time until the next installment. If that time period is too long, you'll move on to other things. With print comics, a month between installments is acceptable. On the internet, if you don't update every week, people forget to come back.

Then I started thinking. Webcomics worked very well because they provided new material for readers to view several times a week: some were daily, others were on a more reasonable Monday/Wednesday/Friday schedule. Would releasing a 30-page manga one page at a time on the web work? Not really, because whatever you put online had to have some sort of reasonable "stopping point" or readers would be confused. Then I wondered if it was possible to do a manga-style story where each page could stand on its own but still form a complete story that flowed from page to page?

Rod suggested we call our webcomic "Megatokyo"--mainly because he owned the domain and wanted to do something cool with it. He suggested that we do a story about two gamers who get stuck in Japan. It would provide a good setup for both of our interests and styles of humor. We'd call the two main characters "Largo" and "Piro," our nicknames at the time which now seem to be stuck to us for the rest of eternity. Rod wrote some scripts, I drew the first two comics, we put them on a temporary website, and I promptly forgot about the whole thing.

After a while Rod started to bug me again. People he showed the comics to seemed to really like them and wanted to see more. I was worried about how long it took to make them; the first two took me at least 12 hours each to sketch, trace, ink, scan and fix up into final comic form. I was a busy architect with a loving girlfriend. I couldn't be spending 36 hours a week doing a webcomic. It wouldn't be fair to Sarah or my sleep schedule.

Since people didn't mind the pencil techniques I used on Fredart, I decided that I could get away without inking the Megatokyo drawings. After all, this was the web, not print. I re-did the first two comics, cutting it down to about eight hours per comic, and then churned out a new design for the website. The next day, Penny Arcade posted a link to us, and I've been trying to keep up with things ever since. To this day, each comic takes from six to eight hours to produce, and I spend far more than 36 hours a week of my free time working on MT-related projects.

The best thing about doing a webcomic is that you can reach a lot of people very efficiently. You don't need to be supported by a big company with lots of money to provide entertainment to a lot of people. That's the real beauty of the web--it's like the ultimate distribution channel for aspiring artists who just want people to experience their work.

What you are holding in your hands is the first printed collection of Megatokyo comics. This book contains what we call "chapter 0," most of the first 133 comics released on the megatokyo.com website in the first year.

Even though we've made the jump to print with this collection, Megatokyo is still and always will be a free online webcomic. Every comic in this book is available on the web. You can go to the website and pick up reading where this book leaves off, even though Volume 2 will be available in March (hint, hint). You can even stay current and read new Megatokyo comics as they come out three times a week (usually).

Crazy? Not really. Megatokyo is what it is because of its webcomic roots. Print versions like this provide higher resolution with edited and corrected strips in a convenient easy-to-read package. I feel that if you like reading Megatokyo, you will enjoy having these print versions. We've tried to add a lot of extras that are not available online. In the end, buying this book helps support the site, and hopefully makes a worthy addition to your bookshelf.

In closing, I just have to say a huge thank you to everyone who has supported and encouraged me over the past two years. Without you, there is no way that I would be where I am today. Most of all, I want to say thank you to Sarah--my conscience, my muse, my angel--for her infinite patience, her love, and her unwavering support. Someone once asked me if she really does have wings like she does in the comic. Yes, she does. You just can't see them.

Fred 'Piro' Gallagher
November 2002

<largo>
My l33t Rant

Although I never imagined it would come this far, our comic has finally made it into print. My goal of wrecking the English language with l33tspeak is finally at hand.

Megatokyo has been a real journey for me in both a professional and creative sense. I remember when I first wanted to do MT back in the spring of 2000. I had tried to start up a few websites, each one meeting with only marginal success. That was when I first approached Fred Gallagher about doing a web-comic. At the time, he already had a site to showcase his art, but had never thought of using webcomics as a medium. He took to the idea slowly, after some coaxing by me. Well, it was more like constant pestering. My original idea was to do a comic about video gamers. After looking around, Fred thought we should do it about both the video game and anime scenes. Our partnership was a unique one. We didn't always agree on things, but looking back on it, I think together we made some real quality material.

So what is in a name? We decided on Megatokyo because I already owned that domain and thought it sounded like it should be the name of an online comic, or at least a band. The name did present a problem because we didn't originally plan for our characters to be in Japan. So we sat down and wrote some scripts to explain the how and why they ended up in Japan, where they continue to be to this day.

At that time, webcomics were just starting to become popular around the net scene. Websites like PVPonline.com, Penny-Arcade.com, and Sinfest.net were the undisputed kings of the domain. Before we had officially launched MT, I sent an email to Jerry Holkins of Penny-Arcade, whom I had been conversing with for awhile, and told him that we were about to start an online comic. So when we did launch, Jerry linked our site and ended up giving us a lot of exposure. We felt we had to keep making MT comics since people were expecting us to produce them at that point. As a result, Jerry had a lot to do with where Megatokyo is today.

Within a few weeks of that first link, we were mentioned on numerous sites. Each day we'd wake up and find out that a website we would patron had decided to plug us instead. It was a hell of a thing. One such link was from another webcomic called PVP, created by Scott Kurtz. My friends and I knew Scott lived in the Dallas, Texas area, and thought it would be fun if we could meet up with him. So a few weeks after MT launched, I decided to email him and offer to treat him to dinner at one of Dallas' premium restaurants, Fogo de Chao. We ended up having a great time, so much that Scott ending up giving us personalized character sketches that he made right there at dinner. It was shortly after then that Scott linked our site. In time, Scott and those of us there that night became friends and ended up regularly gaming together. On that note, if you ever happen see Scott Kurtz, be sure to ask him about Phil the Goblin.

Over time, Fred and I managed to make some new friends in other, much colder places as well. We got to know some of the nice people at my favorite, and very Canadian game company, Bioware. I recall there were some people who thought the only reason I started Megatokyo was so that I could land a job at Bioware. In retrospect, they may have been right. We did end up doing some Bioware/Neverwinter Nights-themed comics for their and our enjoyment. Bioware seemed to get a kick out of them, and their communications director, Brad Grier, linked our comics off their corporate website. He was even nice enough to get us passes to that year's gaming and entertainment trade show, E3 Expo. To top it off, at E3 they let us into the press-only demo of "Neverwinter Nights" and "Star Wars Knights of the Old Republic."

Because of MT, I've attended a lot of conventions to speak at panels, do signings, and just hang out with our readers. There are a lot of convention anecdotes about MT, but due to space limitations, I'll just cover one of my favorites. Larry and Danny are two guys I met at a con because they had constructed a couple of shoulder-mount replicas of our Boo the hamster, and then proceeded to wear them. It was by chance that I passed by and saw a hamster that I knew all too well. It wasn't much later on that the friendship of those two led me to meeting my future wife, and Larry standing as my best man in my wedding.

Ruby is my amazing, patient, supportive, and patient wife. Did I mention she was patient? She has endured evenings of me staring at my computer screen trying to make an unfunny script turn into the coveted funny variety. From weekend long LAN gaming parties to endless hours of online gaming, she has put up with me. She is a real gem, no pun intended, though she will likely hurt me for making that joke.

In retrospect, MT has been more about the people I've met along the way than the work itself. With that in mind, there are a lot of people I'd like to thank for their inspirations, ideas, and support during my time with Megatokyo. Thanks go out to my wife Ruby, Larry Berlin, Jason Coleman, Jonathan Lotman, Bill Lovell, Joe Lynes, Danny McGuire, Kevin Patterson, Matthew Peck, John Schick, Jeff Sheldon, Sterrett Taylor, Matthew Weyandt, Bob McCabe, Brad Grier and all our friends at Bioware, InovaPC.com, So-TrickComputers, and most importantly, all of you reading this. I hope to see all of you again when I finally get rcaston.com up and running. It might even have a new comic on it. Wouldn't that be sw33t?

Rodney "Largo" Caston
November 2002

<dom>
???

What a ride.

Part of me wants to leave it at that, because this entire time I've been preaching economy of language to Fred. Heck, half of me wants to go back two and a half years to fix all the crap I let through in the early days when Rodney and Fred did everything themselves. Nip a sentence here, cut a phrase there, fix up the occasional flopped punch line... But as unhappy as we all are with our own work, it's ours and it's not fair to diddle with what I felt proud of two years ago. I'm still not happy with the NeverQuest punch line, but overall, I'm surprised with how well this little project has done.

I still don't quite know how I got roped into MT-this vessel of collected fantasies in which we have managed to place our hopes and dreams and more than a little of our love. I can't say it was friendship, though friendship was what kept me from laughing at what was then a ludicrous waste of a site from a man-no, not a man, a collection of zeroes and ones without a face who had never been serious before-nor can I call it morbid curiosity, as mere curiosity would have faded long ago, metamorphosing into impatient disgust. Perhaps it was Rodney's force of will-a lust to fulfill this vision from the depths of his turbulent, often seemingly disturbed psyche, a vision so strong, so persistent it drew a neurotic architect and a listless writer toward it, both fully knowing that it would as easily explode as expand, yet unable to pull away from the inexorable will to create. Perhaps it was a moment of weakness, of a hubris, which would not allow for retreat or failure in the face of the jumble of words presented, and would regret the decision at the same time it stubbornly supported it with half-remembered explanations. I suppose it could also have been ego, a wish to see my name entombed in a place where I would be able to point and say This is sprung forth full-grown from my head and the hands of others. It is theirs, and it is mine, sole child of our madness. There is my name, and no one can take it away, not knowing that the name would become shortened, appended, would become its own identity separated by presupposition and perception from a still poorly understood self.

Oh, hell. There I go again, thinking too much about this. What it all boils down to is that Megatokyo has been a load of fun. With the help of Fred and Rod, I've learned about the give-and-take of writing, and about Will Eisner's so-called "sequential art." Or maybe it's that Fred and Rod pointed me to a subject that I have always wanted to learn more about.

It's also been an exercise in separating reality from fantasy, a line blurred by my very presence in pencil and pixel, without the comfort of a pseudonym or alter ego. When Rod first inserted me into the comic, he wrote in his vision of me, and Fred drew it. It is at once an idealized vision of myself and profoundly different from what I want to be. What's a little frightening is that I've leaked into the character as much as he has leaked into me, though I like to think that the vibrating sheep was wholly my idea, a good joke and not some incestuous (or is it autoerotic?) union between Dom the editor (auditor?) and Dom the character.

Yes, Ed and I are like that in real life. No, I don't work at Sega of America, nor do I work at Sega of Japan. Yes, I really do tend to write like this when I'm not constrained by comic strip layouts and the urge to condense my language. And yes, if I could do it all over again, if I could go back to that sunset when Rodney first wrote, "Hey, I have some scripts… could you look at them?"… I wouldn't change a thing. Not even the punch line I always complain about.

What a ride. I hope you enjoy it as much as I have.

Dominic "Dom" Nguyen
November 2002

f r 3 3 t a l k

ONE OF THE PROBLEMS WITH WEBCOMICS IS THAT THE FREEDOM YOU HAVE WITH SIZE AND FORMAT IS BOTH A BLESSING AND A CURSE. FREE FROM THE RESTRICTIONS A PUBLISHER MIGHT PUT ON YOU, YOU CAN DO JUST ABOUT ANYTHING YOU WANT AS LONG AS IT WORKS WITH A WEB BROWSER AND DOESN'T MELT DOWN YOUR SERVER.

THERE IS SOMETHING COSMICALLY AMUSING ABOUT THE PROBLEMS I'VE FACED GETTING MATERIAL READY FOR THIS BOOK. THE FIRST HUNDRED OR SO COMICS WERE DONE IN A SQUARE, FOUR PANEL FORMAT. THEN I HAD THE BRIGHT IDEA TO CHANGE TO A RECTANGULAR, MANGA-STYLE FORMAT. ONLINE, THIS DOESN'T CAUSE ANY PROBLEMS. FOR THE BOOK, IT LEAVES A BIG BLANK SPACE UNDERNEATH THE FIRST HUNDRED OR SO COMICS THAT I NEEDED TO DECIDE HOW TO FILL.

WEBCOMICS ARE DIFFERENT FROM PRINT COMICS BECAUSE THEY ARE A MORE DYNAMIC MEDIUM. EVERY MEGATOKYO COMIC IS ACCOMPANIED BY VARIOUS "RANTS" BY LARGO, DOM, SERAPHIM AND MYSELF. SOME OF THESE MAKE FOR GOOD READING, OTHERS COULD USE TO BE ACCIDENTALLY DELETED. GIVEN THE SIZE OF MY "RANTS" IN PARTICULAR, INCLUDING THEM WOULD MORE THAN DOUBLE THE SIZE OF THIS BOOK --AND WOULD BE A REAL WASTE OF PAPER.

SINCE I'M TOO LAZY TO DRAW NEW MATERIAL AND I CAN PRATTLE ON AIMLESSLY WITH EASE, I'LL USE THIS BLANK SPACE FOR COMMENTS AND OBSERVATIONS.

THIS IS THE FIRST MEGATOKYO COMIC WE EVER DID. IT WAS DONE ALMOST TWO MONTHS BEFORE MEGATOKYO OFFICIALLY LAUNCHED. ORIGINALLY, I WAS GOING TO INK EVERYTHING, BUT CAME TO MY SENSES WHEN I REALIZED HOW LONG THAT WOULD TAKE.

I NEVER INTENDED TO DO MORE THAN ONE OR TWO COMICS. I DID THIS ONE MAINLY TO GET LARGO TO SHUT UP AND LEAVE ME ALONE. HE SEEMED CONVINCED THAT WE SHOULD DO A WEBCOMIC.

THINGS LIKE STORY, ORGANIZATION, OR WHAT WE WERE GOING TO DO NEXT WEEK WERE NOT CONSIDERED VERY IMPORTANT AT THE TIME.

THE ONLY PERSON WHO DIDN'T LAUGH AT US WHEN LARGO ASKED FOR OPINIONS ON SCRIPTS WAS DOM.

WE FIGURED THAT IF WE PUT DOM IN THE STRIP, WE COULD CONTROL HIM BETTER. DOM ACTUALLY TURNED OUT TO BE VERY USEFUL WHEN IT CAME TO CAUSING OUR READERS PAIN.

WE LIKE DOM. IT'S WHY WE KEEP HIM AROUND.

Panel 1:
SO, HOW'D YOU SWING A JOB WITH SEGA JAPAN?

ED AND I BOTH APPLIED RIGHT AFTER COLLEGE.

YOU GUYS WORK TOGETHER?

Panel 2:
NO, THEY ONLY HAD ONE OPENING. YOU REMEMBER HOW COMPETITIVE WE USED TO BE?

Panel 3:
SO, YOU LOCKED YOUR BEST FRIEND IN THE TRUNK OF YOUR CAR SO HE'D MISS THE JOB INTERVIEW...

WHAT ABOUT ALL THE OTHER APPLICANTS?

Panel 4:
WELL, THEY WEREN'T REALLY FRIENDS, YOU KNOW...

CHECK PLEASE.

ODDLY ENOUGH, DOM AND ED HAVE THIS KIND OF RELATIONSHIP IN REAL LIFE.

I FIGURED THAT IT WOULD BE FUN TO USE DOM AND ED TO PLAY ON THE JAPANESE STEREOTYPE THAT ALL AMERICANS ARE WELL-ARMED AND WILLING TO WHIP OUT GUNS AT THE SLIGHTEST PROVOCATION.

THATS A SIG SAUER 9MM DOM IS PACKING—JUST SO YOU KNOW.

I'M TELLING YOU PIRO, IT'S NOT FAIR. I SHOULD BE A GAME DESIGNER.

DUDE, WE'RE IN A HOTEL FULL OF THEM. SEE? OVER THERE IS TRENT OSTER OF BIOWARE.

GO INTRODUCE YOURSELF. A GOOD FIRST IMPRESSION CAN GO A LONG WAY.

PLEASE, MAKE ME YOUR MONKEY BOY!

LARGO'S OBSESSION WITH BIOWARE AND THE GAMES THEY MAKE BORDERS ON THE OBSESSIVE. NO, IT IS OBSESSIVE.

I THINK THAT'S PART OF WHY LARGO IS NOT ALLOWED TO ENTER CANADA ANYMORE.

IDENTIFYING PIRO'S "OBSESSIONS" WAS A BIT HARDER. MOST READERS CAN UNDERSTAND LARGO'S NEED FOR RPGS, FIRST PERSON SHOOTERS, AND OTHER THINGS.

EXPLAINING THE TYPES OF GAMES I LIKE WAS HARDER, SINCE VERY FEW ARE AVAILABLE IN ENGLISH.

LARGO AND I DIDN'T WANT THE HUMOR IN MEGATOKYO TO RELY TOO HEAVILY ON WHAT MIGHT BE CONSIDERED "OBSCURE KNOWLEDGE". THE TRICK IS TO PROVIDE HUMOR ON SEVERAL LEVELS SO THAT EVEN IF YOU DON'T GET ALL OF THE REFERENCES, IT'S STILL FUNNY.

WHAT WOULD A GAMING COMIC BE WITHOUT POKING FUN AT JOHN ROMERO.

I THINK THAT LARGO SPENT MOST OF HIS TIME THINKING ABOUT HOW TO GET US INTO TROUBLE.

"HEY, WE SHOULD HAVE THEM FLY TO JAPAN."

"SURE, OK."

AH, THE DAYS WHEN I DIDN'T WORRY ABOUT SETUP FOR DIRECTIONAL CHANGES IN THE PLOT.

EVEN THOUGH I WASN'T INKING THINGS, EACH COMIC STILL TOOK ABOUT SIX TO EIGHT HOURS TO COMPLETE. PART OF THE REASON IS THAT I SKETCHED EACH FRAME OF THE COMIC FIRST, THEN TRACED THE FINAL VERSIONS ON MARKER PAPER BEFORE I SCANNED THEM IN.

BASICALLY, IT WAS LIKE DRAWING EVERYTHING TWICE. MY SKETCHES WERE WAY TOO MESSY TO USE WITHOUT TRACING THEM FIRST.

THIS IS ARGUABLY THE
MOST WELL-KNOWN COMIC
THAT WE'VE DONE.

IT ALSO MARKS THAT
TERRIBLE DAY WHEN 'L33T
SP34K' ENTERED MY LIFE.

I DIDN'T FULLY GET THE
JOKE UNTIL SOMETIME THE
FOLLOWING WEEK. I'M NOT
WHAT YOU WOULD CALL
"L33T".

IF YOU CAN'T READ WHAT
L33T DUD3 SAYS - DON'T
ASK ME, I HAVE NO IDEA.
ASK LARGO.

THIS EPISODE HAS HAUNTED ME EVER SINCE WE DID IT. I ALWAYS WANTED TO MAINTAIN SOME SORT OF LOOSE REALISM IN MEGATOKYO.

LARGO JUST GOT INTO JAPAN BY BEATING A NINJA AT A "MORTAL COMBAT" CONSOLE GAME.

THERE GOES THAT PLAN.

THIS WAS WHEN WE STARTED TO SEE THAT SOME OF OUR IDEAS WERE GOING TO CONFLICT WITH EACH OTHER'S STORY CONCEPTS. I WANTED TO LEAN TOWARDS A MORE STRUCTURED STORY, LARGO WANTED THINGS MORE FREE-FLOWING.

OK, THAT WAS FUN. I DON'T KNOW WHAT THIS THING IS, BUT IT SURE IS COOL.

TOLDYA. I GUESS WE SHOULD LOOK INTO GETTING HOME.

<I'M SORRY, BUT YOUR CARD HAS BEEN REJECTED.>

<WHAT?>

WHAT DID SHE SAY?

UH... MY CREDIT CARD MUST BE MAXED OUT. GIMME YOURS.

ARE YOU KIDDING? I JUST MAXED OUT MY CARD GETTING THIS THING.

THEN WE HAVE A PROBLEM.

ARE YOU TELLING ME THAT WE'RE STUCK HERE?

WELL...

HOLD VERY STILL. I THINK I JUST FIGURED OUT A USE FOR THIS THING.

HAVING SPENT A FEW WEEKS IN JAPAN MYSELF, I KNOW VERY WELL HOW EASY IT IS TO SPEND A LOT OF MONEY VERY QUICKLY.

ALSO, WE ARE INTRODUCED TO LARGO'S "COOL THING" WHICH IS... WELL... WE DON'T REALLY KNOW YET.

AS SOON AS WE DO, IT'LL BE AVAILABLE IN OUR ONLINE STORE IN LESS THAN TWO WEEKS. GOD BLESS AMERICA.

THIS IS JUST GREAT. THOUSANDS OF MILES FROM HOME, NO MONEY, NO PLACE TO STAY, AND WORST OF ALL, I'M GOING TO MISS THE RELEASE OF "BALDUR'S GATE 2". SOMEONE PLEASE SHOOT ME.

DON'T FREAK ON ME. I KNOW A BUNCH OF PEOPLE HERE IN TOKYO. IT SHOULDN'T BE TOO HARD TO FIND A PLACE TO CRASH.

THEN WHY ARE WE SITTING HERE? I'M STARVING, AND I NEED TO CHECK MY EMAIL.

WELL...

ON THE PLANE, I WAS FINALLY ABLE TO FINISH "WITH YOU MITSUMETEITAI" WITH MANAMI. UNFORTUNATELY, IT SEEMS TO HAVE DRAINED THE BATTERY ON MY LAPTOP. I CAN'T GET AT MY ADDRESS BOOK.

YOU'RE DOING THIS ON PURPOSE, AREN'T YOU?

RELAX. I'M SURE WE'LL BE BACK BEFORE "NEVERWINTER NIGHTS" IS RELEASED.

GREAT. THAT'LL BE WHAT, THREE YEARS?

NIGHT SCENES ARE HARD TO DO IN PENCIL, SO I EXPERIMENTED WITH SHADING IN PHOTOSHOP TO GET THE RIGHT FEEL.

LARGO'S OBSESSION WITH A CERTAIN BIOWARE GAME STARTS TO SURFACE AGAIN. AND AGAIN.

THIS JOKE MAKES LITTLE SENSE UNLESS YOU'RE FAMILIAR WITH THE ANIME SERIES "MARTIAN SUCCESSOR NADESICO".

COSPLAY, IF YOU ARE NOT FAMILIAR WITH THE TERM, IS WHERE YOU DRESS UP AS YOUR FAVORITE ANIME OR GAME CHARACTER. IT'S A COMMON PRACTICE AT ANIME CONVENTIONS BOTH HERE AND IN JAPAN.

WELL, THIS IS SHINJUKU. MY FRIEND TSUBASA LIVES AROUND HERE SOMEWHERE.

WONDERFUL. I AM IN AWE OF YOUR USELESSNESS.

MAYBE IF I GET ONLINE, I'LL BE ABLE TO GET A HOLD OF HIM.

<piro> tsubasa!
<tsubasa> hello! How are you?
<piro> well, I'm standing in a Gateway Country store in Shinjuku.
<tsubasa> ... what? You are in Japan?
<piro> yeah. I need a favor. We need a place to crash.

<SIR, WHAT ARE YOU DOING??>

<HELP! FIRE!!>

<AIEEEE!!>

<tsubasa> ah... let me guess, Largo-san is with you.
<piro> uh, yeah. Could you hurry?

TSUBASA, A FRIEND OF MINE IN JAPAN, HELPED ME WORK OUT WHERE MOST OF THE EVENTS IN MEGATOKYO TAKE PLACE.

LIKE MANY PEOPLE WHO SPEND A LOT OF TIME ONLINE, A GOOD CHUNK OF MY SOCIAL INTERACTION WITH PEOPLE IS ON IRC. IN FACT, LARGO AND I DO NOT LIVE ANYWHERE NEAR EACH OTHER, SO EVERYTHING WE DID WAS VIA IRC AND INSTANT MESSAGING.

tok tok

tok tok

HAVING AN AMD CHIP THAT USED TO OVERHEAT WITHOUT ANY OVERCLOCKING WHATSOEVER, I FOUND THIS COMIC TO BE PARTICULARLY HUMOROUS.

AND YES, LARGO HAS ACTUALLY HAD SMALL FIRES ERUPT INSIDE HIS COMPUTER CASES.

I DON'T REALLY KNOW WHY, BUT I WAS OK WITH THE CONCEPT OF LARGO GETTING HIT BY A BUS.

LARGO'S ABILITY TO ABSORB ALMOST CARTOONISH LEVELS OF VIOLENCE WAS ONE OF THE BENEFITS OF THE DUAL NATURE OF THE WORLD THAT WAS STARTING TO DEVELOP.

ONE THING I WANTED TO MAKE SURE OF IN MEGATOKYO WAS THAT IF SOMEONE GETS HURT, THEY STAY HURT. LARGO'S ARM WON'T MAGICALLY HEAL ITSELF IN THE NEXT COMIC.

LARGO DOES MANAGE TO HEAL PRETTY FAST THOUGH. FAST, BUT NOT INSTANTLY.

I'M SORRY YOU HAVE HAD SO MANY PROBLEMS SINCE YOU ARRIVED. JAPAN IS NOT A DANGEROUS COUNTRY, YET YOU HAVE ALREADY BEEN HURT!

MY PLACE IS VERY SMALL AND VERY MESSY, BUT YOU ARE WELCOME TO STAY. I HOPE IT WILL NOT BE TOO UNCOMFORTABLE.

IT IS SO EXCITING THAT YOU HAVE FINALLY COME TO JAPAN, PIRO-SAN! WE MUST CELEBRATE!

PIRO-SAN?

LARGO-SAN?

UH OH...

JAPAN IS A PRETTY SAFE PLACE TO WANDER AROUND AIMLESSLY.

I ALWAYS FELT SAFE NO MATTER WHERE I WAS. BUT THEN AGAIN, I WASN'T LOOKING FOR TROUBLE WHEN I WAS THERE.

tak tak

tak tak

MUCH OF THE TIME, LARGO AND PIRO DON'T ACKNOWLEDGE THE EXISTENCE OF EACH OTHER, EXCEPT AS A SOURCE OF MINOR IRRITATION.

OTHER TIMES, THEY ARE VERY MUCH IN SYNCH WITH EACH OTHER'S THOUGHTS. IT'S AN INTERESTING RELATIONSHIP.

THE NUMBER OF PEOPLE WHO EMAIL ME SAYING "MY FRIEND IS JUST LIKE LARGO AND I'M JUST LIKE PIRO!" MAKES ME WORRY ABOUT THE WORLD.

IT'S AMAZING HOW A BAD HAIR CUT CAN RUIN A COOL CHARACTER.

POOR LARGO. OF COURSE, HIS HAIR IS BIGGER IN THE OPPOSITE DIRECTION. I WONDER WHAT THEY CALL THAT?

DISDAIN FOR GRAVITY, USUALLY.

I CAN'T HELP BUT CHUCKLE AT THE CONCEPT OF A FORCE FEEDBACK 'DATING SIM' GAME.

IMAGINE HOW BRUISED YOU'D GET.

- Piro's Bad Art Day -

YO. PIRO HERE. I'M SURE YOU'VE NOTICED THE LACK OF REFINEMENT AND SKETCHY NATURE OF TODAY'S STRIP. THIS IS WHAT THEY LOOK LIKE BEFORE I CLEAN THEM UP.

"BAD ART DAYS" ARE FOR WHEN I JUST DON'T HAVE TIME TO DO A NORMAL STRIP. THERE ARE A LOT OF THINGS THAT CAN CAUSE THIS.

FOR INSTANCE, I COULD COME DOWN WITH A BAD COLD. FRIENDS & FAMILY COULD STOP BY TO VISIT.

I COULD HAVE A DEADLINE AT WORK THAT REQUIRES ME TO SPEND MANY LONG EVENINGS AT THE OFFICE...

... OR MY COPY OF "AIR" COULD FINALLY ARRIVE.

DUDE, COULD YOU AT LEAST FINISH DRAWIN' MY HANDS? I'M GONNA DROP MY BEER.

MY FIRST DEAD PIRO DAY. YOU CAN SEE WHY I WAS TRACING MY SKETCHES AT THE TIME - EVEN THOUGH THEY WERE GETTING BETTER.

WITH ALL THE TIME IT TOOK TO MAKE THESE COMICS - SIX TO EIGHT HOURS - IT'S NO WONDER THAT I MISSED A DAY OR TWO,

A CLASSIC LARGO MOMENT.

NOTE THAT WHEN YOU SEE BRACKETS LIKE <THESE>, IT MEANS THE CHARACTER IS SPEAKING IN JAPANESE.

I DON'T THINK THAT ERIKA'S LINE WOULD BE VERY HARD TO UNDERSTAND IN ANY LANGUAGE.

IT TOOK A WHILE FOR THE GIRLS TO START SHOWING UP IN MEGATOKYO, MAINLY BECAUSE I FELT THAT I DIDN'T HAVE THE SKILLS TO DRAW THE FEMALE CAST PROPERLY.

IT WOULD BE ANOTHER SIX MONTHS BEFORE I FELT THAT I DID.

WHY DO I ALWAYS SHOW
THE PEOPLE WHO WORK AT
THESE SHOWS WEARING
BASEBALL CAPS?

HMM, NO IDEA.

ODDLY ENOUGH, WE DIDN'T MAKE THIS UP.

YOU REALLY CAN GET THINGS LIKE THIS FROM VENDING MACHINES IN JAPAN. WE DIDN'T EVEN MENTION THE WEIRD STUFF.

KIMIKO'S COMMENT HERE IS A SETUP FOR THINGS THAT HAPPEN IN LATER STRIPS. WHEN WRITING SCRIPTS, YOU CAN DO SUBTLE THINGS NOW THAT LATER BECOME THE FOCUS OF A JOKE OR STORY ARC.

NOTE THAT THIS IS THE FIRST TIME PIRO MEETS KIMIKO.

IN MEGATOKYO, THE BASIC PREMISE IS THAT LARGO EXISTS TO ABSORB PHYSICAL DAMAGE, WHILE PIRO EXISTS TO TAKE EMOTIONAL DAMAGE.

AS THIS PARTICULAR COMIC DEMONSTRATES, THIS ISN'T ALWAYS THE CASE.

I DON'T ALWAYS DRAW THE ENTIRE FRAME IN ONE DRAWING. FOR INSTANCE, THE GIRLS IN THE FOREGROUND ARE DRAWN SEPARATELY FROM LOCKERS IN THE BACKGROUND

POOR KIMIKO, THE GIRL DOES HAVE HER PROBLEMS.

SINCE I'M ACTUALLY
AN ARCHITECT, NOT A
COMIC ARTIST, DRAWING
BUILDINGS AND STUFF
COMES NATURALLY.

I LIKE TO USE DYNAMIC
"CAMERA ANGLES" WHEN
I CAN, ESPECIALLY WHEN IT
HELPS CUT DOWN ON HOW
MUCH OF THE CHARACTERS
I HAVE TO DRAW.

THE TABLE THEY ARE SITTING AT IS A "KOTATSU" – A FOLDING TABLE WITH A LITTLE ELECTRIC HEATER UNDER IT.

IF YOU AREN'T USED TO SITTING ON THE FLOOR LIKE THIS, IT REALLY DOES HURT AFTER A WHILE.

THIS IS THE FIRST COMIC WHERE I USED THE ORIGINAL SKETCHES AND DIDN'T TRACE OVER THEM. I WAS GETTING MUCH BETTER AT DRAWING THINGS WITH FEWER SCRIBBLES AND CONSTRUCTION LINES. I FIGURED THAT IF I COULD SKIP RE-TRACING, I COULD SPEND MORE TIME ON THE FRAMES THEMSELVES.

YOU ALWAYS LOSE SOMETHING WHEN YOU TRACE AN ORIGINAL SKETCH. BY ELIMINATING THIS STEP, IT GETS CLOSER TO THE DRAWING WHERE I FIRST PUT PENCIL TO PAPER.

I THINK THAT THIS EVENTUALLY LED TO BETTER LOOKING AND MORE EXPRESSIVE COMICS.

SERAPHIM, WHO HAS A MEDICAL BACKGROUND, TOLD ME THAT IT WOULD TAKE ABOUT SIX WEEKS FOR LARGO'S BROKEN ARM TO HEAL.

THAT SOUNDED LIKE A GOOD STRETCH OF TIME BEFORE TSUBASA'S PATIENCE WORE OUT. TSUBASA IS VERY PATIENT.

SOMETIMES FRIENDS CAN'T TAKE SUBTLE HINTS, OR EVEN DIRECT ONES.

I HAVE HEARD STORIES FROM JAPANESE FRIENDS WHO REFER TO SOME OF THEIR AMERICAN VISITORS AS BEING "AS BAD AS PIRO AND LARGO".

YOU HAVE NO IDEA HOW BAD I FEEL FOR THEM.

IT WAS SERAPHIM'S IDEA THAT SHE WOULD MAKE A GOOD CONSCIENCE FOR PIRO IN THE COMIC. SHE'S A TOUGH TALKING LITTLE ANGEL THAT TRIES TO KEEP PIRO STRAIGHT, BUT HAS AS MUCH LUCK AS THE REAL SERAPHIM DOES WITH ME.

SERAPHIM IS MY GIRLFRIEND AND FIANCEÉ IN REAL LIFE, IN CASE YOU DIDN'T GUESS.

THIS WAS A RATHER SAD COMIC BECAUSE ONE OF SERAPHIM'S CATS, BULLITO, HAD DIED THE PREVIOUS DAY. I WANTED TO HAVE SOME SORT OF MEMORIAL FOR HER, SO THIS IS WHAT I DID.

AH, RANDOM, SENSELESS VIOLENCE.

SINCE SO MUCH VIOLENCE ON TV AND IN THE MOVIES IS SENSELESS, DOESN'T IT MAKE SENSE THAT DOM AND ED CAN PRACTICE VIOLENCE THAT MAKES NO SENSE?

WOW, I'M AMAZED THAT YOU WERE ABLE TO GET DOM AND ED TO SEND US SOME MONEY TO GET HOME.

WELL, I GOT SOME DIRT ON BOTH OF THEM. THEY USUALLY COUGH UP WHEN I REMIND THEM.

NOW ALL WE GOTTA DO IS GO BUY SOME PLANE TICKETS.

SURE, BUT LETS GET A FEW BEERS FIRST. THIS BAR HERE IS OPEN!

LARGO, NO! WE BARELY HAVE ENOUGH MONEY TO GET THE TICKETS!!

WE CAN'T SPEND ANY OF THE MONEY ED AND DOM SENT US, OR WE WON'T BE ABLE TO...

...AFFORD...

...THE TICKETS...

AH... WHY ARE YOU STILL HERE?

HE'S HOME. DID WE EVER DECIDE WHAT WE WERE GONNA TELL HIM?

AWW, JUST GET HIM A FEW BEERS AND SHOW HIM SOME OF THE CRAP YOU GOT IN THAT GAME STORE. HE'LL BE FINE.

TRUE.

I SOMETIMES WONDER WHAT IT IS THAT LARGO HAS ON DOM AND ED THAT CAN MAKE THEM PONY UP CASH LIKE THAT.

WAIT, THOSE TWO PHOTOGRAPHS... OK, NEVER MIND.

LIES! ALL LIES! YOU CAN'T PROVE THAT'S ME BEHIND THE EWE.

tak tak

tak tak

I RESISTED DOING THIS COMIC BECAUSE I DIDN'T WANT TO CONDONE DRUG USE OF ANY SORT. I DON'T CONSIDER IT A LAUGHING MATTER.

IT DOES, HOWEVER, MAKE SOCIAL COMMENTARY ON VARIOUS LEVELS, SO I WENT WITH IT.

NOTE THAT THIS IS THE FIRST TIME THAT PIRO AND LARGO SEPARATE - PIRO GOES OUT AND LEAVES LARGO BEHIND.

THIS SUCKS. TSUBASA'S MAD AT ME. LARGO'S USELESS. I'M SURE HE'LL MANAGE TO BURN DOWN THE APARTMENT BEFORE I GET HOME. WHY AM I ALWAYS THE ONE WHO HAS TO FIX THINGS? WHAT THE HELL DID I EVER DO?

WHAT AM I SAYING? THIS IS ALL MY FAULT. I'M THE ONE WHO DRAGGED LARGO HERE. WHAT WAS I THINKING? HAS MY LIFE BECOME SO DEVOID OF MEANING THAT THE ONLY THING THAT MATTERS IS HAVING ENOUGH GAMES TO KEEP MYSELF EMOTIONALLY AFLOAT? HAVE I BECOME THAT PATHETIC?

本
BOOKS

少女まんが
GIRLS COMICS

SHOUJO MANGA HAS HELPED ME WITH SO MANY PROBLEMS. ALL I NEED TO DO IS READ UNTIL I FIND A SIMILAR SITUATION AND IT WILL TELL ME EVERYTHING I NEED TO KNOW.

SHOUJO MANGA, OR "GIRLS COMICS", TEND TO HAVE LESS VIOLENCE AND DEEPER STORYLINES THAN SHOUNEN MANGA OR "BOYS COMICS".

IT'S NOT UNUSUAL FOR GUYS TO READ SHOUJO MANGA, BUT MOST WOULDN'T BE CAUGHT DEAD BROWSING THE SHOUJO MANGA SECTION OF THE LOCAL BOOKSTORE.

tak
tak

tak
tak

HIBIKI-SAN CAN'T UNDERSTAND WHY TOORI HATES HER. SHE LATER DISCOVERS THAT IT WAS BECAUSE HER FATHER, WHO LEFT HER MOTHER WHEN SHE WAS YOUNG BECAUSE HE WAS GAY, HAD RUN OFF WITH TOORI'S FATHER WHICH LEAD TO HIS MOTHER COMMITTING SUICIDE...

(SIGH) THAT DOESN'T HELP, EVEN THOUGH HER FATHER DOES LOOK A BIT LIKE LARGO.

KAMI IS GIVEN A MAGIC STICK BY PAUPAU, HER CUTE LITTLE STUFFED ANIMAL. SHE FINDS THAT WITH IT SHE CAN TURN HERSELF INTO 'MAGICAL STUFFED KAMI-CHAN'. SHE USES HER NEWFOUND ABILITIES TO HELP HER BEST FRIEND WITH A BOY SHE LIKES. SOON, HOWEVER, SHE FINDS THAT SHE HAS FALLEN IN LOVE WITH THIS BOY HERSELF...

HM, A LITTLE CLOSER, BUT IT STILL DOESN'T HELP.

YUKI IS A JR. HIGH SCHOOL GIRL WHO FALLS IN LOVE WITH HER ENGLISH TEACHER, A SHY AMERICAN WITH BLOND HAIR WHO IS MUCH OLDER THAN HER. SHE IS VERY STUBBORN AND DOES EVERYTHING SHE CAN TO WIN HIM, WHICH LEADS TO A TRAGIC ENDING WHERE THEY BOTH DIE SEPARATE, VIOLENT DEATHS...

YEAH, I WISH. THAT AIN'T EVEN CLOSE...

‹SEE YUKI? I TOLD YOU! SHE'S BEEN HERE FOR HOURS. SHE'S READ JUST ABOUT EVERYTHING ON THE SHELVES! ISN'T SHE CUTE?›

‹ASAKO, I THINK THAT'S A 'HE'.›

‹NO WAY! YOU THINK?›

WHAT'S SCARY ABOUT THIS COMIC IS THAT THESE SCENARIOS ARE NOT VERY FAR OUTSIDE OF WHAT YOU REALLY FIND IN SOME SHOUJO MANGA STORIES.

FOR THE RECORD, PIRO IS A GUY. HE ALWAYS HAS BEEN, ALWAYS WILL BE. SHEESH.

tak tak

tak tak

YUKI IS A FUN CHARACTER. I WANTED HER TO BE A "JAPANESE SCHOOL GIRL" THAT WAS CLOSER TO BEING A REAL JAPANESE SCHOOL GIRL THAN THE SORT OF FANCIFUL CHARACTERS YOU SEE IN MOST ANIME AND GAMES.

WHEN I WAS IN JAPAN, I ACTUALLY DID KNOCK OVER A DISPLAY IN THE SHOUJO MANGA SECTION OF A BOOKSTORE WITH MY BOOK BAG. NO ONE HELPED ME PICK IT UP, THOUGH.

THAT... THAT... THAT WAS SO EMBARRASSING.

GOD, MY CHEST HURTS.

IDIOT! IDIOT!! WHY DID I RUN AWAY? I SPEAK AND READ JAPANESE BETTER THAN MOST AMERICANS. WHY DIDN'T I JUST TALK TO THEM? WHAT THE HELL IS THE MATTER WITH ME?

THEY PROBABLY THINK I'M JUST SOME DORKY STUPID IDIOT FANBOY NOW.

MAYBE... I SHOULD GO BACK. ALL THEY DID WAS ASK ME WHAT I WAS DOING. I DIDN'T NEED TO FREAK OUT LIKE THAT. THEY **DID** HELP ME PICK UP THAT DISPLAY I KNOCKED OVER.

ACTUALLY... THEY WERE KINDA CUTE. REAL, HONEST TO GOODNESS JAPANESE SCHOOL GIRLS. PENNY-LOAFERS, FLOPPY SOCKS....

click

(AHEM)...

I THINK IT'S TIME WE HAD A LITTLE TALK.

LARGO IS THE KIND OF PERSON WHO WILL FALL DOWN A FLIGHT OF STAIRS, RUN BACK UP, AND FALL RIGHT DOWN AGAIN.

PIRO SITS AT THE BOTTOM OF THE STAIRS AND WONDERS IF THEY ARE SAFE TO CLIMB OR NOT.

HE'S A LOT LIKE ME, HE THINKS TOO MUCH.

tak tak

tak tak

OK, FANTASY OVER.

DO YOU KNOW HOW OLD THOSE GIRLS ARE?

UH.... HIGH SCHOOL? SEVENTEEN?

TRY FIFTEEN. YOU GRADUATED FROM COLLEGE LAST YEAR. DO THE MATH.

BUT, BUT, I WASN'T...

DON'T 'BUT' ME, MISTER MAN. CHASING FIFTEEN YEAR OLD GIRLS IS WRONG, AND YOU KNOW IT.

I'VE OVERLOOKED A LOT OF PROSECUTABLE OFFENSES RECENTLY. TRICKING POOR DRUNKEN LARGO INTO COMING TO JAPAN. MAXING OUT YOUR CREDIT CARDS. TAKING ADVANTAGE OF YOUR FRIEND TSUBASA, SPENDING DOM AND ED'S MONEY ON TOYS, NOT TICKETS.

BUT I CAN'T OVERLOOK YOU PURSUING HIGH SCHOOL AGED GIRLS.

DON'T BLAME ME! IT'S YEARS OF ANIME AND GAMES FULL OF HIGH SCHOOL GIRLS THAT HAS PROGRAMMED ME TO BE ATTRACTED TO THEM!! I CAN'T HELP IT! IT'S NOT MY FAULT!

SO, YOU'RE SAYING IF LARGO WENT AROUND TOWN SHOOTING PEOPLE, THAT WOULD BE OK BECAUSE HE'S BEEN PLAYING FIRST PERSON SHOOTER GAMES FOR YEARS?

THAT'S TOTALLY DIFFERENT.

NO IT'S NOT, FREAK BOY.

THE ARGUMENT THAT VIOLENT VIDEO GAMES LEAD TO VIOLENT BEHAVIOR ALSO EXISTS IN JAPAN WHERE IT IS SOMETIMES APPLIED TO "DATING SIM" STYLE GAMES.

TO ME, YOU CAN NEITHER CONDONE NOR EXCUSE YOUR BEHAVIOR BASED ON THE GAMES YOU PLAY.

THERE IS NOTHING WRONG WITH ESCAPISM AS LONG AS IT DOESN'T GO TOO FAR. IN FACT, YOU CAN ARGUE THAT A CERTAIN AMOUNT OF IT IS HEALTHY AND NORMAL.

tak tak

tak tak

I'M NOT SAYING ANIME AND GAMES ARE BAD. SOMETIMES EVEN I'VE ENJOYED THEM.

I DON'T WANT TO BE A HARDASS. BUT YOU'VE GOT TO SHAPE UP. YOU'RE STUCK IN A FOREIGN COUNTRY WITH NO MONEY AND NO WAY OF GETTING HOME. YOU DON'T HAVE TIME FOR MORAL DILEMMAS.

YOU'RE THE ONE WHO GOT YOURSELF INTO THIS MESS. LARGO CAN'T EVEN HOLD A JOB BACK HOME, NEVER MIND HERE. YOU HAVE TO FIND A JOB AND EARN ENOUGH MONEY TO BUY TWO TICKETS HOME.

YEAH, I KNOW.

NO MORE GAMES, NO MORE ANIME, NO MORE HIGH SCHOOL GIRL FANTASIES. PLAYTIME IS OVER. DO YOU UNDERSTAND?

OK! SO, FIND A JOB, EARN SOME MONEY, AND THEN WE GO HOME, RIGHT?

YUP! THAT'S THE PLAN!

YAY! GO PIRO! GAN-BA-TTE! WAI!

AND NO FLIRTING WITH SCHOOL AGE GIRLS?

NOPE! I PROMISE! I'LL STAY AWAY FROM ANY GIRL UNDER FIFTY!

‹HE FORGOT HIS BAG?›

‹LOOKS LIKE HE DID. I WONDER HOW WE CAN RETURN IT TO HIM?›

‹YUKI-CHAN, YOUR DAD IS A POLICE OFFICER, RIGHT? MAYBE HE CAN HELP!›

YOU HAVE TO BE CAREFUL AND REMEMBER WHERE YOUR FANTASIES LIE IN RELATION TO REALITY.

BECAUSE YOU NEVER KNOW WHEN SOMEONE ELSE'S FANTASY MIGHT INVOLVE *YOU*.

tak   tak

tak

THIS IS AN IMPORTANT COMIC BECAUSE BY THIS POINT, WE HAD FIGURED OUT HOW LARGO'S REALITY AND PIRO'S REALITY COULD COEXIST.

TWO YEARS LATER, WE ACTUALLY TESTED THE "HEAVY OBJECT" THEORY WHEN LARGO AND I PARTED WAYS AND I WENT SOLO WITH MEGATOKYO.

IT'S WEIRD HOW FRAME 3 IS AS IMPORTANT TO MEGATOKYO AS FRAME 2 IS....

KIMIKO SURE IS CUTE IN THAT DEJIKO OUTFIT...

TO ANSWER A LONG STANDING QUESTION ABOUT THIS EPISODE:

YES, THAT IS MILK. NO THAT ISN'T CEREAL. IT'S RAMEN. LARGO IS POURING MILK OVER A BOWL OF INSTANT RAMEN. I THINK HE BLEW OUT HIS TASTE BUDS YEARS AGO.

OK, THIS ONE IS JUST WEIRD.

I DON'T KNOW HOW I GOT TALKED INTO PUTTING ALF IN THERE...

LARGO AND I WERE HUGE "EXCEL SAGA" FANS BACK IN '99-00. THIS IS THE MOST OBVIOUS EVIDENCE – THERE'S MORE, IF YOU LOOK FOR IT.

‹DON'T WORRY SO MUCH, ASAKO. I DON'T THINK THERE'S ANYTHING WE CAN DO TONIGHT. YES, I'LL TALK TO MY DAD ABOUT IT. NO, I AM NOT GOING TO GO THROUGH THE BOOK BAG. YES, I PROMISE.›

‹UH HUH, SURE. OK, G'NIGHT›

‹LET'S SEE... LOOKS LIKE A SKETCHBOOK.›

‹WOW. THESE ARE GOOD. A FOREIGNER WHO CAN DRAW LIKE THIS? I WONDER WHO HE IS?›

‹I GOTTA SHOW THIS TO ASAKO AND MAMI...›

‹OH, WAIT, I BETTER NOT. WE AGREED NOT TO GO THROUGH HIS STUFF. ASAKO WOULD BE REALLY MAD AT ME IF SHE KNEW. I WAS SUPPOSED TO JUST BRING IT HOME AND GIVE IT TO MY DAD.›

‹YEAH, LIKE THE POLICE WILL DO ANYTHING ABOUT IT.›

‹EEEP.›

‹IF THEY SAW THIS, THEY MIGHT DO SOMETHING ABOUT IT.›

‹I GUESS I WON'T BE SHOWING THIS TO DAD.›

I LOVE THE WAY YUKI IS TELLING ASAKO THAT SHE WON'T GO THRU PIRO'S BOOK BAG, AT THE SAME TIME SHE IS PULLING HIS STUFF OUT TO LOOK AT IT.

YUKI'S ABILITY TO LIE WITH A COMPLETELY STRAIGHT FACE MAKES ME REALLY WONDER ABOUT HER.

tak tak tak tak

I CAN'T BELIEVE I LOST MY BOOK BAG. WHAT AN IDIOT. WHAT AM I GONNA DO? THERE ARE A LOT OF IMPORTANT THINGS IN THAT BAG I DON'T WANT TO LOSE. WHERE DID I LEAVE IT?

WAITAMINUTE... THAT BOOKSTORE I WAS IN MOST OF THE AFTERNOON. I KNOW I HAD MY BAG WHEN I KNOCKED THE DISPLAY OVER. YEAH, I DID. I THINK I MUST HAVE LEFT IT BEHIND AFTER THOSE GIRLS HELPED ME FIX THE DISPLAY.

ACK!! THOSE GIRLS! WHAT IF THEY HAVE MY BOOKBAG? WHAT IF THEY FIND MY SKETCHBOOK?!? OHMYGOD, OHMYGOD, OHMYGOD...

RELAX, RELAX, DON'T PANIC. THIS IS JAPAN. PEOPLE HERE ARE OVERLY COURTEOUS AND POLITE.

I'M SURE THEY JUST TOOK IT UP TO THE COUNTER FOR ME TO GET LATER. THERE'S NO WAY THEY WOULD GO THROUGH IT OR FIND MY SKETCHBOOK. THERE'S NOTHING TO WORRY ABOUT.

<"Very nice drawing. But I think the bra looks uncomfortable. The straps are too far apart.">

HEHEH.

I'D BE HORRIFIED IF ANYONE GOT A HOLD OF ONE OF MY SKETCHBOOKS.

tak tak   tak tak

‹THIS ISN'T ANYTHING LIKE THE PERVERTED STUFF MY BROTHER DRAWS. SURE, SOME OF THE GIRLS HE'S DRAWN ARE JUST WEARING UNDERWEAR, BUT IT'S NOT LIKE WEIRD STUFF. MOST OF THE GIRLS ARE WEARING PRETTY COOL CLOTHES. INTERESTING.›

‹OI, I'M GONNA BORROW YOUR DREAMCAST. MINE'S ON THE FRITZ.›

FWAP!

‹BROTHER! GET OUT! AND NO, YOU CAN'T BORROW IT!›

‹WHY NOT? YOU AREN'T USING IT.›

‹'CAUSE I SAID SO!›

‹WHATEVER.›

bop!

‹IF YOU AREN'T OUT OF MY ROOM IN 10 SECONDS, MOM IS GOING TO 'ACCIDENTALLY' DISCOVER THAT STASH OF 'ADULT' GAMES HIDDEN IN THE BACK OF YOUR CLOSET.›

‹HEY, CHILL, I'M GOIN'...›

I WANTED YUKI'S BROTHER TO BE MORE INTERESTING THAN JUST SOME FACELESS BACKGROUND CHARACTER.

OF COURSE, ONCE THEY WERE DEVELOPED, THE ENTIRE SONODA FAMILY TURNED OUT RATHER INTERESTING.

EVIDENCE OF PIRO'S OBSESSION WITH "SAINT TAIL".

tak tak tak tak

JUNPEI WAS JUST TOO COOL A CHARACTER TO NOT BRING BACK AT SOME POINT.

JUNPEI, THE L33T NINJA. YOU KNOW IT HAD TO HAPPEN.

ONE OF THE FIRST SCRIPTS I EVER TRIED TO WRITE FOR MT WAS "JUNPEI STRIKES BACK". OBVIOUSLY, IT DIDN'T GET OFF THE GROUND, BUT IT WAS THE FIRST TIME I REALLY GOT INVOLVED IN MT.

I'M NEVER GONNA FIND THAT BOOKSTORE AND I'M NEVER GONNA GET MY BOOK BAG BACK. IT'S GONE. I GIVE UP.

IT'S MORNING ALREADY. I BETTER GET BACK TO THE APARTMENT.

AW, MAN, I NEED A NEW RAIL CARD. I'VE USED THIS ONE UP. I HOPE I HAVE ENOUGH TO GET A NEW ONE. IT'S A LONG WALK TO KICHIJOUJI FROM HERE.

WHEW. JUST ENOUGH. I'LL BE ABLE TO GET AROUND TOKYO FOR A FEW MORE DAYS, BUT I DON'T EVEN HAVE ENOUGH MONEY LEFT TO BUY A CAN OF MILK COFFEE. I'M BEGINNING TO HATE THIS PLACE.

LIKE EVERYTHING ELSE IN MY LIFE, THIS WHOLE TRIP IS A POINTLESS WASTE. I WANNA GO HOME.

I JUST DON'T CARE ANYMORE.

<OHMYGOD, WHERE'S MY RAIL CARD? WHERE'S MY CHANGE PURSE?>

THIS IS THE POINT WHERE I STARTED TO GET INTO TROUBLE.

LIFE ISN'T ALWAYS FUNNY. USUALLY YOU CAN FIND HUMOR IN JUST ABOUT EVERYTHING.

WHEN I STARTED MEGATOKYO, I FELT THAT THERE WOULD BE TIMES WHEN IT WOULD NOT BE PARTICULARLY FUNNY.

BUT SOMETIMES THINGS AREN'T FUNNY AT ALL.

LIFE DOESN'T ALWAYS
HAVE A PUNCH LINE.

<SIR...>

<I... I CAN'T TAKE YOUR CARD... PLEASE...>

<SIR?>

A LOT OF PEOPLE EMAILED ME WONDERING WHAT THE JOKE WAS IN THE PREVIOUS COMIC. IT WAS VERY FRUSTRATING.

I WAS TRYING TO BREAK OUT OF THE MOLD THAT WEBCOMICS HAD TO BE LIKE NEWSPAPER COMICS - SOMETHING FUNNY, EVERY DAY.

SOME PEOPLE WERE UNWILLING TO ACCEPT THAT, AND EVEN THREATENED TO STOP READING IF I PULLED SOMETHING LIKE THAT AGAIN.

MY RESPONSE WAS SIMPLE - FINE, DON'T READ IT. NO ONE IS FORCING YOU.

WHY DID I DO THAT? I'M SURE SHE DIDN'T EVEN USE IT. SHE PROBABLY JUST TOSSED IT IN THE TRASH.

(SIGH)

IT'S A REALLY LONG WALK TO KICHIJOUJI FROM HERE.

I JUST CAN'T GET OVER HOW DENSELY PACKED EVERYTHING IS HERE IN JAPAN. CARS, TRAINS, BUILDINGS, PEOPLE. IT'S ALL CRAMMED TOGETHER.

IT'S LIKE THERE'S NO ROOM FOR ANYTHING THAT DOESN'T FIT.

I SUPPOSE I HAVE THIS FANTASY THAT I 'FIT IN' BETTER HERE THAN I DO BACK HOME.

THE TRUTH IS, I DON'T BELONG HERE ANY MORE THAN LARGO DOES.

WOW. LOOK AT ALL THE TRACKS. THIS MUST BE THE INOKASHIRA LINE, WHICH ENDS AT KICHIJOUJI STATION.

I WISH LIFE HAD MULTIPLE SAVE POINTS LIKE GAMES DO. IT'D BE EASIER TO GO BACK AND FIX MAJOR SCREW-UPS.

I'D JUST HAVE TO MAKE SURE I 'SAVE' EVERY FIVE MINUTES.

LARGO WAS GETTING ON MY CASE ABOUT THE FACT THAT PIRO WAS GETTING WAY TOO MOPEY AND INTROSPECTIVE.

WELL, THAT'S JUST HOW PIRO IS. IT'S ALMOST AS ANNOYING AS LARGO AND HIS "L33T SP33K".

THE LITTLE CHARACTER IN THE UPPER RIGHT FRAME IS HOMAGE TO A NOW-GONE JAPANESE WEBCOMIC THAT HELPED INSPIRE ME TO DO MEGATOKYO. THAT LITTLE FISH THING IS A TAIYAKI, A KIND OF HOT PASTRY.

tak tak

tak tak

<IT WAS AWFUL. I COULDN'T FIND MY RAIL CARD AND I WAS REALLY LATE. I DIDN'T KNOW WHAT TO DO. I GUESS I WAS STARTING TO PANIC.>

<AND THEN, OUT OF THE BLUE THIS GUY HANDS ME A BRAND NEW 3000 YEN RAIL CARD AND WALKS OFF. HE DISAPPEARED BEFORE I COULD EVEN SAY "NO".>

<I MEAN, I COULDN'T ACCEPT SOMETHING LIKE THAT FROM A TOTAL STRANGER.>

<IT'S ALMOST LIKE HE KNEW I WOULDN'T TAKE IT IF HE GAVE ME THE CHANCE TO RESPOND. IN FACT, I STILL DON'T FEEL RIGHT ABOUT HAVING USED IT.>

<I HAVE NO IDEA HOW I CAN PAY HIM BACK FOR THE CARD. I HAVE NO IDEA WHO HE WAS.>

<EXCELLENT, NANASAWA-SAN! I LIKE IT! A LITTLE WISTFUL, A LITTLE WHINY. KINDA CHEERY, KINDA SOMBER. WONDERFUL ACTING>

<WE'LL BE CONTACTING YOU.>

<UHM... WAS THIS ON?>

<I WASN'T ACTING, I WAS JUST TALKING. I MEAN...>

KIMIKO IS AN ASPIRING "SEIYUU", OR VOICE ACTRESS. IN JAPAN, ANIME FANS OFTEN WORSHIP SEIYUU MORE THAN THE CHARACTERS THEY PLAY.

OF COURSE, KIMIKO IS STILL TRYING TO BREAK INTO THE BUSINESS. IT'S A COMPETITIVE INDUSTRY, AND I'VE BEEN DOING A LOT OF RESEARCH TO HOW THE INDUSTRY WORKS SO THAT I CAN REPRESENT IT ACCURATELY.

tak tak

tak tak

OK, THIS ISN'T THE COMIC I WAS PLANNING TO DO TODAY. WHY? BECAUSE FOR SOME REASON, THE ABILITY TO DRAW COMPLETELY ABANDONED ME THIS EVENING. IT'S CALLED 'ARTIST'S BLOCK,' AND IT SUCKS.

AFTER THREE HOURS OF WASTING PERFECTLY GOOD PAPER, I GAVE UP. I STARTED THINKING... PERHAPS I'VE ALWAYS HAD 'ARTIST'S BLOCK' AND WAS JUST TOO STUPID TO REALIZE IT.

MAYBE, I DIDN'T LOSE THE ABILITY TO DRAW, JUST MY DELUSION THAT I *COULD* DRAW IN THE FIRST PLACE.

IN FACT, JUST ABOUT EVERYTHING IN THIS STUPID SKETCHBOOK IS UNWORTHY. IT WOULD BE BETTER TO ADD A LITTLE WARMTH TO THIS COLD WORLD BY BURNING IT ALL...

OH, THE DRAMA...

≡CLICK≡

Y'KNOW, THIS 'TORTURED ARTIST' ROUTINE IS GETTING OLD.

NOW STOP BEING A DUMBASS AND GIVE ME BACK MY LIGHTER BEFORE YOU HURT YOURSELF.

UHM, SORRY, MY BAD.

I STARTED TO USE THIS DRAWING STYLE FOR "REAL LIFE ADVENTURES OF PIRO AND SERAPHIM" COMICS.

OFTEN OUR OWN EXPERIENCES AND INTERACTIONS CAN BE FAR MORE ENTERTAINING THAN ANYTHING I CAN MAKEUP. YES, WE ARE REALLY LIKE THAT.

tak tak

tak tak

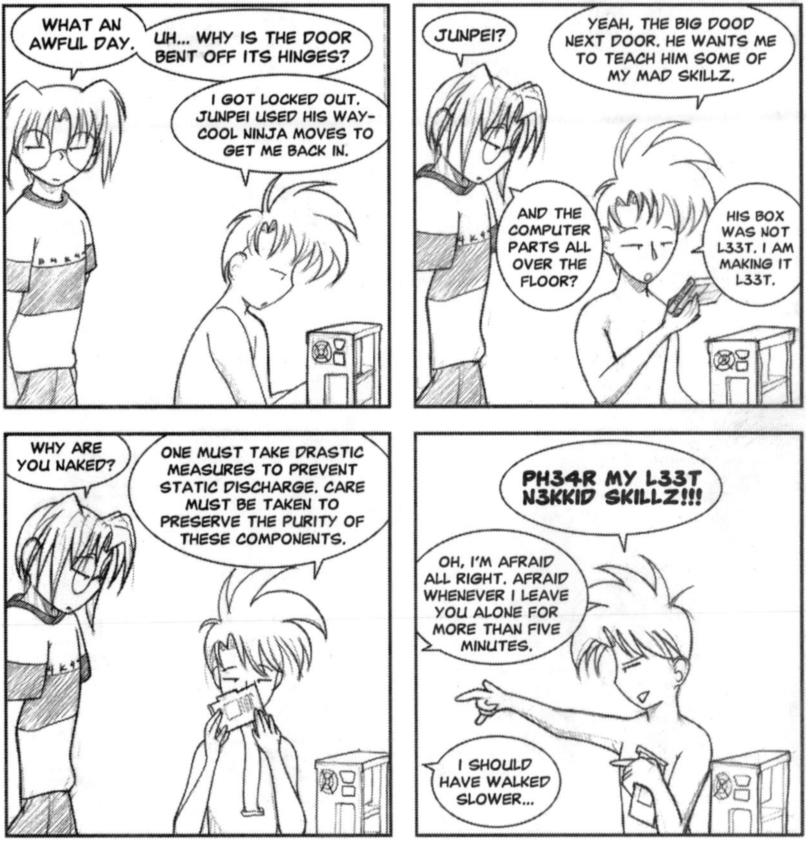
WHAT AN AWFUL DAY.
UH... WHY IS THE DOOR BENT OFF ITS HINGES?
I GOT LOCKED OUT. JUNPEI USED HIS WAY-COOL NINJA MOVES TO GET ME BACK IN.
JUNPEI?
YEAH, THE BIG DOOD NEXT DOOR. HE WANTS ME TO TEACH HIM SOME OF MY MAD SKILLZ.
AND THE COMPUTER PARTS ALL OVER THE FLOOR?
HIS BOX WAS NOT L33T. I AM MAKING IT L33T.
WHY ARE YOU NAKED?
ONE MUST TAKE DRASTIC MEASURES TO PREVENT STATIC DISCHARGE. CARE MUST BE TAKEN TO PRESERVE THE PURITY OF THESE COMPONENTS.
PH34R MY L33T N3KKID SKILLZ!!!
OH, I'M AFRAID ALL RIGHT. AFRAID WHENEVER I LEAVE YOU ALONE FOR MORE THAN FIVE MINUTES.
I SHOULD HAVE WALKED SLOWER...

GOD, THIS ONE SCARES ME.

I'M SORRY, BUT IT DOES. I CAN'T DEAL WITH THE IMAGERY.

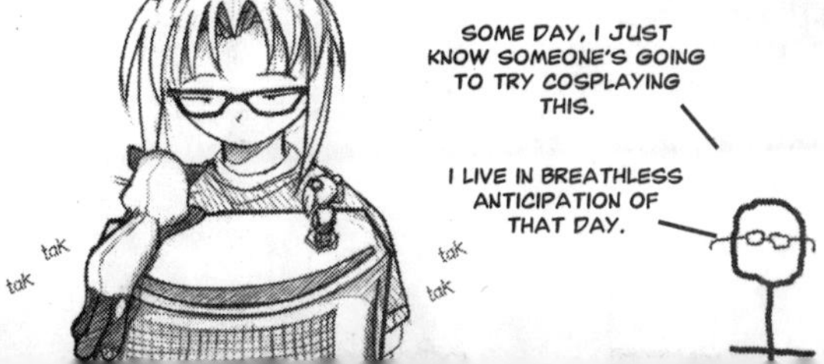
SOME DAY, I JUST KNOW SOMEONE'S GOING TO TRY COSPLAYING THIS.
I LIVE IN BREATHLESS ANTICIPATION OF THAT DAY.
tak tak
tak tak

SOME PEOPLE HAVE OFTEN WONDERED IF ERIKA AND KIMIKO ARE SISTERS. THEY AREN'T, THEY ARE JUST FRIENDS AND ROOMMATES. I LAY THE BLAME FOR THIS CONFUSION ON THE PROBLEMS I HAD DRAWING THEM TOO SIMILARLY IN EARLY COMICS LIKE THIS ONE.

ONE COOL THING ABOUT ERIKA IS THAT SHE'S SO POKER-FACED YOU NEVER KNOW IF SHE IS SERIOUS OR NOT.

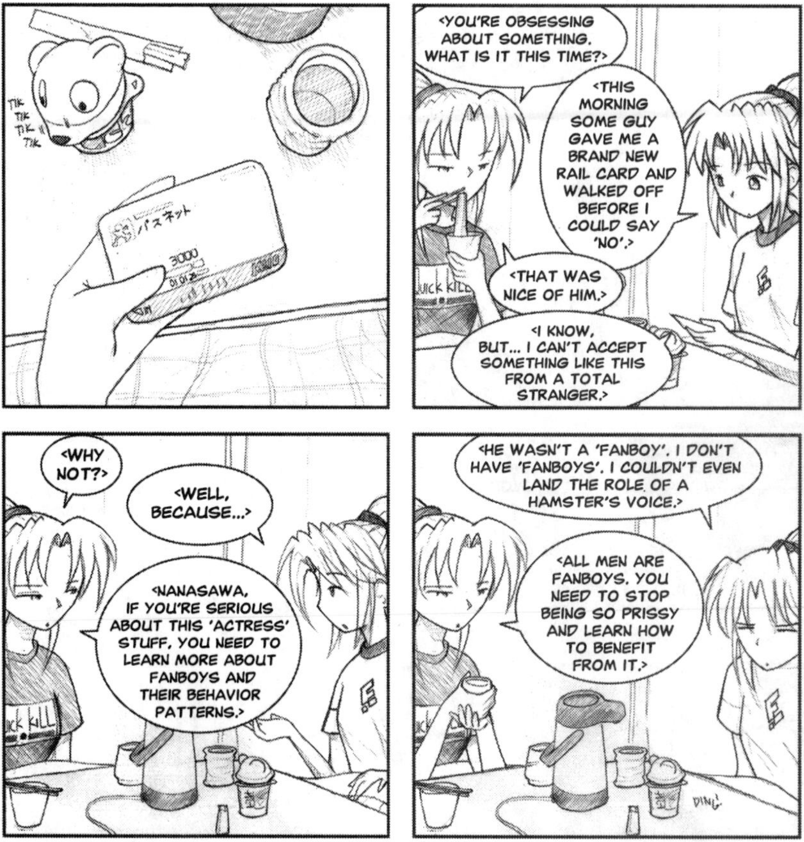
TIK
TIK
TIK
TIK
パスネット
3000
<YOU'RE OBSESSING ABOUT SOMETHING. WHAT IS IT THIS TIME?>
<THIS MORNING SOME GUY GAVE ME A BRAND NEW RAIL CARD AND WALKED OFF BEFORE I COULD SAY 'NO'.>
<THAT WAS NICE OF HIM.>
<I KNOW, BUT... I CAN'T ACCEPT SOMETHING LIKE THIS FROM A TOTAL STRANGER.>
<WHY NOT?>
<WELL, BECAUSE...>
<NANASAWA, IF YOU'RE SERIOUS ABOUT THIS 'ACTRESS' STUFF, YOU NEED TO LEARN MORE ABOUT FANBOYS AND THEIR BEHAVIOR PATTERNS.>
<HE WASN'T A 'FANBOY'. I DON'T HAVE 'FANBOYS'. I COULDN'T EVEN LAND THE ROLE OF A HAMSTER'S VOICE.>
<ALL MEN ARE FANBOYS. YOU NEED TO STOP BEING SO PRISSY AND LEARN HOW TO BENEFIT FROM IT.>
DING!

PIRO AND LARGO AREN'T THE ONLY CHARACTERS IN MEGATOKYO THAT ARE OBSESSIVE. KIMIKO HAS PLENTY OF HER OWN LITTLE QUIRKS.

SHE HAS A LOT OF TROUBLE ACCEPTING THINGS FROM OTHER PEOPLE. MOST PEOPLE WOULD SHRUG THIS OFF, BUT KIMIKO IS THE TYPE THAT JUST WON'T LET GO.

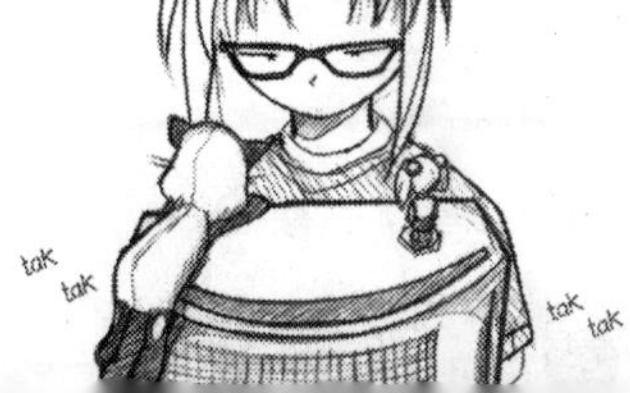
tak
tak
tak
tak

LOOK FAMILIAR? MOST OF MY FRIENDS HAVE A ROOM OR TWO THAT LOOKS LIKE THIS.

IT'S HARD DOING A COMIC ABOUT GAMERS WHEN THEY DON'T HAVE A COMPUTER TO PLAY ON, SO WE TOOK SOME LIBERTIES TO GET LARGO AND PIRO "GEARED UP."

SOMETIMES OUR EXPERIENCES IN A GAME CAN BE JUST AS IMPORTANT AS OUR REAL LIFE EXPERIENCES, SO IT'S ONLY NATURAL TO SHOW PIRO AND LARGO IN THE GAMES THEY PLAY.

PIRO IS ONE OF THOSE GAMERS WHO PREFERS TO USE FEMALE CHARACTERS WHEN PLAYING. "PIROKO" CAN KICK LARGO'S ASS IN QUAKE 3 - A FACT THAT IRRITATES LARGO TO NO END.

IN JAPAN, MOST ANIME FANS SPEND A LOT OF TIME LEARNING HOW TO DRAW THEIR FAVORITE ANIME CHARACTERS. THE WEB IS FULL OF WEB PAGES AND GALLERIES OF THEIR WORK.

MY OWN ART SITE, FREDART.COM, IS INSPIRED BY THIS GENRE OF JAPANESE WEBSITES.

EMAIL HAS ALWAYS BEEN
A PROBLEM FOR ME.
EVEN WHEN I USED TO GET
A REASONABLE AMOUNT
OF IT, I WAS BAD AT
RESPONDING.

THESE DAYS, I CAN'T EVEN
KEEP UP WITH READING IT
AS IT COMES IN.

"DUMB AS DRIVEWAY
GRAVEL."... HEHEH.
I KNOW PEOPLE LIKE THAT.

LARGO THOUGHT THAT IT WASN'T FAIR THAT PIRO HAD A CONSCIENCE BUT LARGO DID NOT. HE SUGGESTED THAT HIS CONSCIENCE COULD BE A LOT LIKE THE LITTLE SPACE HAMSTER STAR FROM ONE OF BIOWARE'S POPULAR GAMES. (IT'S AN OBSESSION, I TELL YOU!)

SINCE A HAMSTER REALLY DID SEEM APPROPRIATE FOR LARGO'S CONSCIENCE, BOO - COMPLETE WITH STRAP-ON WINGS AND FRESH FROM A TEMP AGENCY - ARRIVED TO SEE WHAT HE COULD DO.

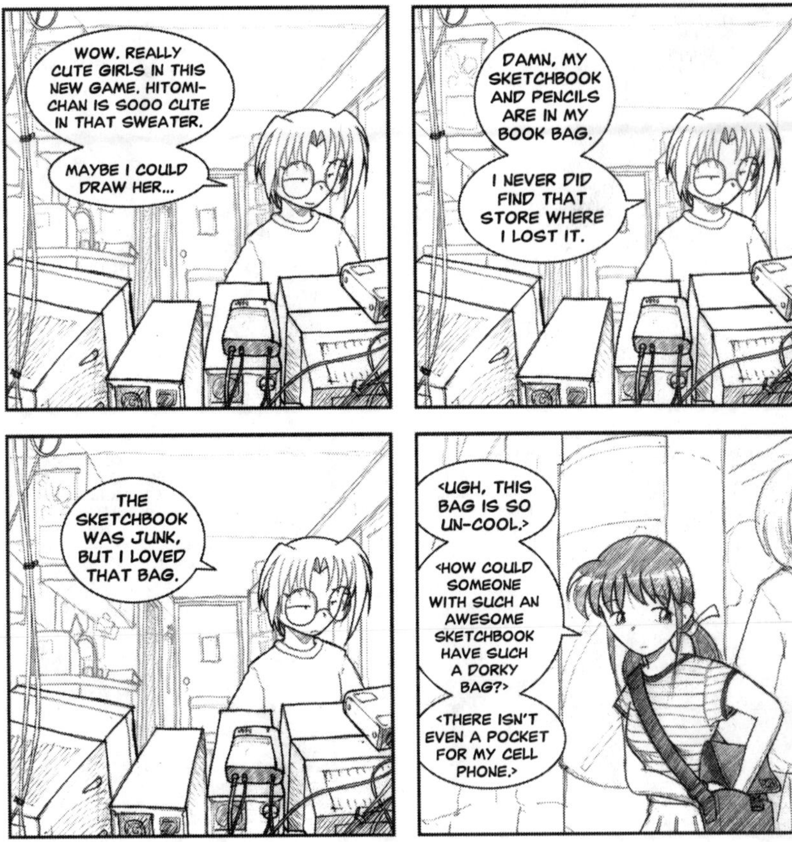
WOW. REALLY CUTE GIRLS IN THIS NEW GAME. HITOMI-CHAN IS SOOO CUTE IN THAT SWEATER.
MAYBE I COULD DRAW HER...
DAMN, MY SKETCHBOOK AND PENCILS ARE IN MY BOOK BAG.
I NEVER DID FIND THAT STORE WHERE I LOST IT.
THE SKETCHBOOK WAS JUNK, BUT I LOVED THAT BAG.
<UGH, THIS BAG IS SO UN-COOL.>
<HOW COULD SOMEONE WITH SUCH AN AWESOME SKETCHBOOK HAVE SUCH A DORKY BAG?>
<THERE ISN'T EVEN A POCKET FOR MY CELL PHONE.>

A LOT OF YOU ARE PROBABLY WONDERING, "WHAT IS YUKI THINKING?"

NEVER UNDERESTIMATE A PLUCKY 15-YEAR-OLD. SHE PROBABLY DOESN'T KNOW EITHER.

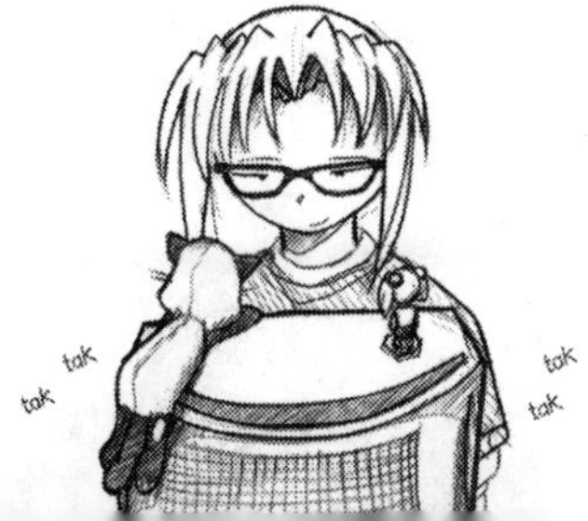
tak
tak
tak
tak

‹YUKI, MAMI, LOOK!! MORE TEDDY BEARS!!›

‹WE'LL WAIT HERE. I'VE SEEN MORE TEDDY BEARS THAN I CAN DEAL WITH TODAY.›

‹'KAY!!›

‹THAT GIRL JUST NEVER RUNS OUT OF ENERGY.›

‹YEAH, IT'S ONE OF THE THINGS I LIKE ABOUT HER.›

‹TOO BAD SHE'S SO GULLIBLE.›

‹GULLIBLE?›

‹FOR INSTANCE, SHE BELIEVED YOUR STORY ABOUT BUYING A BOOK BAG JUST LIKE THE ONE YOUR FATHER 'RETURNED' TO THAT AMERICAN GUY.›

‹PERSONALLY, I'D LIKE TO KNOW WHAT WAS IN THAT BAG THAT SPURRED THIS LITTLE CHARADE.›

‹IF I ASKED ASAKO, I'M SURE SHE WOULD GLADLY MAKE YOUR LIFE HELL 'TIL YOU TOLD US EVERYTHING.›

‹YOU WOULDN'T DARE...›

‹SO, YOU'RE BUYING US LUNCH? I THINK ICE CREAM WOULD BE NICE, TOO.›

‹HAVE I EVER MENTIONED THE THINGS I **DON'T** LIKE ABOUT **YOU**?›

WE ALL HAVE FRIENDS WE CAN HIDE THINGS FROM, AND FRIENDS WHO CAN SEE RIGHT THROUGH US.

I FEEL FOR YOU IF YOU HAVE TOO MANY OF THE LATTER.

tak tak

tak tak

<(SIGH)>

<I WISH MAMI WOULD JUST LEAVE ME ALONE.>

<"OHHH! YOU HAVE A CRUSH ON HIM, DON'T YOU?">

<UH HUH, YEAH RIGHT. WHATEVER.>

<HOW COULD I HAVE A 'CRUSH' ON HIM? I DON'T KNOW ANYTHING ABOUT HIM.>

<NOTHING AT ALL.>

<EXCEPT FOR HIS DRAWINGS. ALL THE GIRLS HE DRAWS ARE SO... SAD.>

<IT'S LIKE YOU CAN FEEL HOW UNHAPPY HE IS. LIKE HE HAS SOME SORT OF INNER TURMOIL, SOME KIND OF INNER PAIN THAT HE EXPRESSES IN HIS ART.>

<I JUST... I WISH I KNEW WHY HE WAS SO SAD.>

<I GUESS I'LL NEVER KNOW.>

MAN, THIS IS SO SAD. I CAN'T EVEN AFFORD A NEW SKETCHBOOK. WHAT A LOSER.

CHARACTER PLACEMENT IS PROBABLY ONE OF THE HARDEST THINGS ABOUT WRITING A COMIC LIKE THIS.

YOU HAVE TO PLAN FAR IN ADVANCE TO GET CHARACTERS TO BE IN THE RIGHT PLACE AT THE RIGHT TIME.

WRITING IS AN ORGANIC PROCESS, AND THE STORY CAN TAKE ON A LIFE OF ITS OWN IF YOU AREN'T CAREFUL.

tak tak

tak tak

NOTE THAT WE ARE STARTING TO SEE THE BREAKDOWN OF THE FOUR-PANEL SETUP.

ONE OF THE HARDEST THINGS ABOUT DOING MEGATOKYO IS THAT I'M TRYING TO DO SEQUENTIAL COMICS WHERE EACH EPISODE HAD TO STAND ON ITS OWN. THE LATEST COMIC IS ALWAYS A STOPPING POINT.

AT ABOUT THIS TIME I WAS REALLY STARTING TO HAVE TROUBLE WITH THE LIMITATIONS OF THE ONE-TWO-THREE-FOUR COMIC SETUP.

I STARTED THINKING ABOUT CHANGING FORMAT.

WHY IS SHE WEARING MY BOOK BAG? I CAN'T BELIEVE SHE'D JUST KEEP IT. THAT'S PRETTY COLD.

WHAT'D SHE DO? JUST THROW OUT ALL MY STUFF?

OH MAN, SHE'S COMIN' THIS WAY!

OH WOW. THAT WAS CLOSE.

<YOU MUST BE THE NEW MASCOT. GOOD TIMING, I NEED A BREAK.>

WHAT'S SAD IS THE REAL VERSION OF THAT HAT IS WAY TO SMALL TO ACTUALLY FIT ON A GROWN UP'S HEAD.

HALF THE FUN OF THIS COMIC WAS DRAWING ALL THE LITTLE DOLLS ON THE SHELF. OH, AND ERIKA'S OUTFIT, TOO.

tak tak   tak   tak

PERSONALLY, I THINK THAT BOO IS ABOUT AS EFFECTIVE WITH LARGO AS ANY CONSCIENCE WOULD BE.

POOR BOO. HE TRIES.

‹THE BOSS IS STILL AT LUNCH, SO YOU'RE THE ONLY ONE HERE.›

‹WATCH THE STORE. I'LL BE RIGHT BACK.›

‹UH... OH... SURE...›

I WONDER...

YEAH... IT COULD WORK.

MAYBE I REALLY COULD WORK HERE. IT'S NOT LIKE I DON'T KNOW THIS STUFF. HECK, I KNOW THEIR STOCK AS WELL AS ANYONE, MAYBE BETTER.

I FEEL GOOD ABOUT THIS.

I THINK EVERYTHING IS GONNA BE OK.

‹RELAX, ASAKO, WE'LL GET LUNCH NEXT! I JUST WANTED TO COME BACK HERE AND GET THAT CD I WANTED.›

I PATTERNED THE "MEGAGAMERS" STORE AFTER SOME OF THE SMALL ANIME AND GAME SHOPS YOU CAN FIND IN AND AROUND TOKYO.

THE STORE IS ACTUALLY TWO LEVELS IN A SMALL BUILDING WITH A STORAGE ROOM ON THE TOP FLOOR.

tak tak

tak tak

GIVEN THE REAL LIFE RELEASE SCHEDULE OF THE COMIC BEING TWO TO THREE COMICS PER WEEK, PEOPLE WERE GETTING IRRITATED WITH HOW LONG IT TOOK FOR THINGS TO HAPPEN.

MOST READERS FOLLOWING THE COMIC BACK THEN DIDN'T HAVE THE LUXURY OF READING ALL OF THE EARLIER COMICS IN A ROW LIKE THIS.

THE STREETS OF TOKYO HUM WITH LIFE AND ACTIVITY. EACH DAY, THOUSANDS OF PEOPLE LIVE OUT THE LITTLE DRAMAS THAT MAKE UP THEIR LIVES. TO THEM, THEY HAVE NOTHING TO FEAR, EXCEPT THEIR OWN PROBLEMS.

LITTLE DO THEY REALIZE HOW QUICKLY THINGS COULD CHANGE...

ABOUT THIS TIME, I STARTED TO GET REALLY BUSY AT WORK, AND I WAS FINDING MYSELF SHORT ON TIME, SO I EXPERIMENTED WITH SOME SINGLE FRAME STRIPS.

THE MOST AMUSING THING ABOUT THIS COMIC IS LARGO'S T-SHIRT, WHICH WAS JUST A RANDOM SKETCH AT THE TIME. PEOPLE ALMOST THREATENED BODILY HARM IF WE DIDN'T MAKE T-SHIRTS WITH "3VIL L33T" ON THEM.

ONLY LARGO COULD FIND AN ANCIENT CAVE OF EVIL IN DOWNTOWN TOKYO.

OBVIOUSLY, BOO IS DOING A STELLAR JOB OF KEEPING LARGO OUT OF TROUBLE.

I COULD PROBABLY DO A WHOLE SERIES OF COMICS ABOUT YUKI AND HER FRIENDS.

YUKI IS THE LEADER OF THIS LITTLE CLUSTER, BUT THE ARRIVAL OF PIRO AND HIS BOOK BAG HAS STIRRED THINGS UP. THIS IS WHY HER FRIENDS AREN'T GIVING HER ANY SLACK.

SOMETHING DARKLY CUTE
THIS WAY COMES.

PEOPLE ON THE FORUMS
SPENT MONTHS JUST
WONDERING WHAT HER
NAME WAS.

YOU WILL NEVER SEE
PIRO IN A DRESS.

CROSSDRESSING COSPLAY
== THE EVIL.

SHE'S THE SOURCE OF THE EVIL. I KNOW IT.

SQUEEK!

WE NEED GUNS, BOO. LOTS OF GUNS.

PERKIGOTH? QUEEN OF THE UNDEAD? OR JUST A GIRL WHO LIKES TO MESS WITH LARGO'S HEAD?

OH, AND PEOPLE TELL ME THAT IT'S REALLY HARD TO GET HAIR RIBBONS TO DO THAT.

THE AMAZING THING IS THAT PEOPLE DO IT ANYWAY, JUST TO LOOK LIKE MIHO.

tak tak

tak tak

‹I CAN'T REMEMBER WHAT TIME ERIKA SAID SHE GETS OFF WORK TODAY.›

‹I HOPE SHE'S NOT TOO BUSY. I NEED TO TALK TO HER.›

(SIGH...)

‹HOW DO I GET MYSELF INTO THESE SITUATIONS?›

I·A·C
I AM CUTE

MOST "ONE PANEL" COMICS DIDN'T WORK AS WELL AS "THE LITTLE DRAMAS" STRIP DID, SO I TRIED TO THINK OF OTHER WAYS TO SAVE TIME WHEN I WAS SWAMPED.

THERE IS SOMETHING REALLY WRONG WITH THIS DRAWING, THE PROPORTIONS ARE ALL SCREWED UP.

I REALLY HAVE TO REDRAW THIS STRIP SOMEDAY.

tak tak

tak tak

THIS WAS A FUN STRIP. I LIKE THE WAY LARGO'S MIND JUMPS FROM THOUGHT TO THOUGHT.

I GUESS A SHARPENED PENCIL COULD TECHNICALLY BE CONSIDERED A "WOODEN STAKE" IN A PINCH.

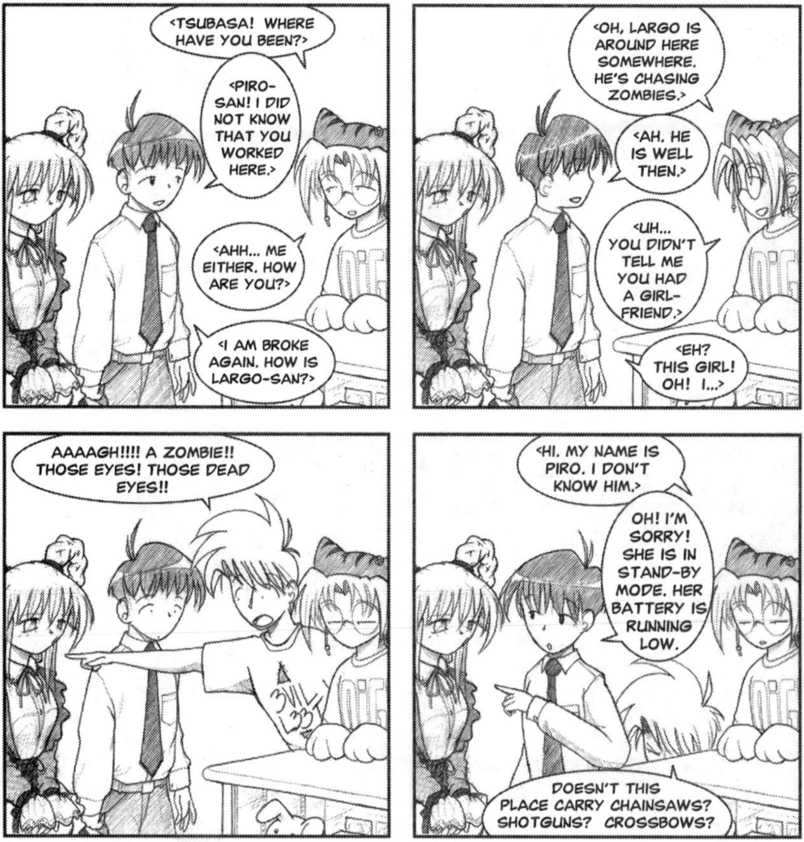
<TSUBASA! WHERE HAVE YOU BEEN?>
<PIRO-SAN! I DID NOT KNOW THAT YOU WORKED HERE.>
<AHH... ME EITHER. HOW ARE YOU?>
<I AM BROKE AGAIN. HOW IS LARGO-SAN?>
<OH, LARGO IS AROUND HERE SOMEWHERE. HE'S CHASING ZOMBIES.>
<AH. HE IS WELL THEN.>
<UH... YOU DIDN'T TELL ME YOU HAD A GIRL-FRIEND.>
<EH? THIS GIRL! OH! I...>
AAAAGH!!!! A ZOMBIE!! THOSE EYES! THOSE DEAD EYES!!
3VIL L33T
<HI. MY NAME IS PIRO. I DON'T KNOW HIM.>
OH! I'M SORRY! SHE IS IN STAND-BY MODE. HER BATTERY IS RUNNING LOW.
DOESN'T THIS PLACE CARRY CHAINSAWS? SHOTGUNS? CROSSBOWS?

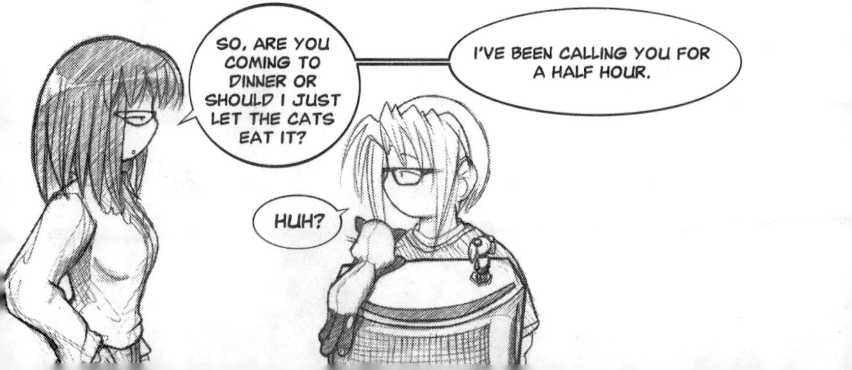
SO, ARE YOU COMING TO DINNER OR SHOULD I JUST LET THE CATS EAT IT?
I'VE BEEN CALLING YOU FOR A HALF HOUR.
HUH?

<YOU BOUGHT A ROBOT GIRL??>

<NO, SHE IS A PLAY-STATION 2 ACCESSORY. PING-CHAN IS A PROTO-TYPE. I HAVE INVESTED IN THE PROJECT.>

<THE PROJECT?>

<THE SONY SEVS-44936 WILL WORK WITH ANY GAME THAT USES THE EMOTIONAL DOLL SYSTEM (EDS).>

<SHE IS A NON-H MODEL, AND WILL ONLY WORK WITH PURE GAMES.>

<AS A RESULT, SHE IS VERY SHY AND INSISTS ON HER PRIVACY.>

<'EDS' ALLOWS HER TO ACTUALLY BECOME ONE OF THE GIRLS IN THE GAME. ELEMENTS OF THESE GIRLS WILL BE ABSORBED INTO HER BASIC PERSONALITY PATTERNS.

<OVER TIME, SHE WILL BECOME AN AMALGAMATION OF ALL THE GIRLS IN ALL THE DATING SIMULATIONS AND VISUAL NOVELS YOU PLAY.>

<SHE COMES WITH A FREE COPY OF "PRINCESS MAKER" - IT'S HER FAVORITE GAME.>

<WOW. LARGO WAS RIGHT, SHE REALLY IS CAPABLE OF DEVOURING YOUR SOUL!>

<ISN'T SHE WONDER-FUL?>

<CAN I PLAY WITH HER WHEN YOU ARE DONE?>

I'M SORRY, I WASN'T PAYING ATTENTION.

WHAT ELSE IS NEW?

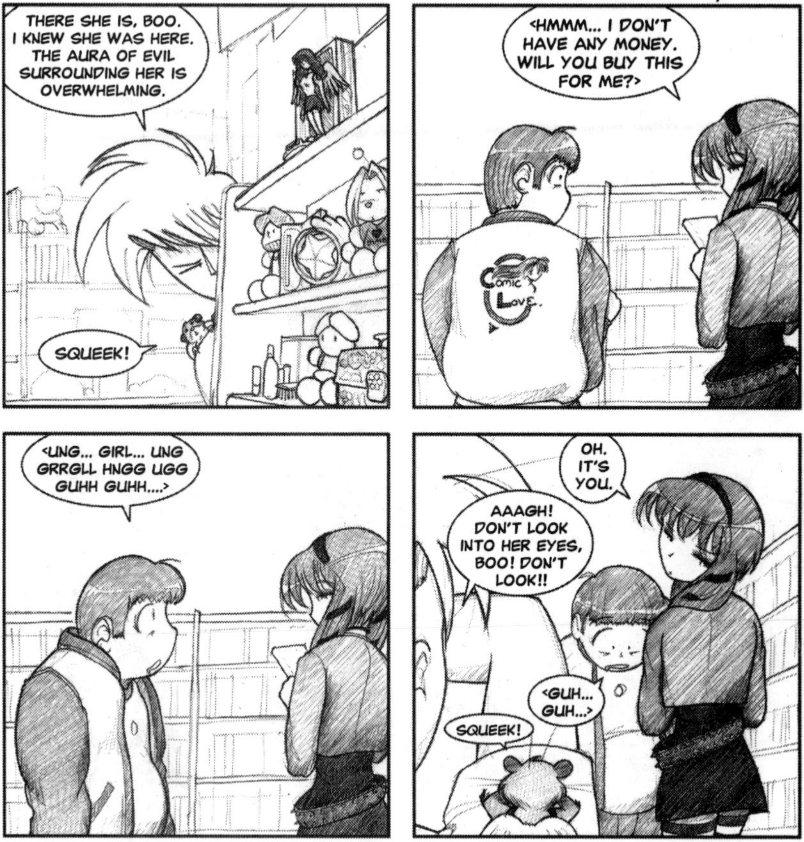
THERE SHE IS, BOO. I KNEW SHE WAS HERE. THE AURA OF EVIL SURROUNDING HER IS OVERWHELMING.
SQUEEK!
<HMMM... I DON'T HAVE ANY MONEY. WILL YOU BUY THIS FOR ME?>
<UNG... GIRL... UNG GRRGLL HNGG UGG GUHH GUHH....>
OH. IT'S YOU.
AAAGH! DON'T LOOK INTO HER EYES, BOO! DON'T LOOK!!
<GUH... GUH...>
SQUEEK!

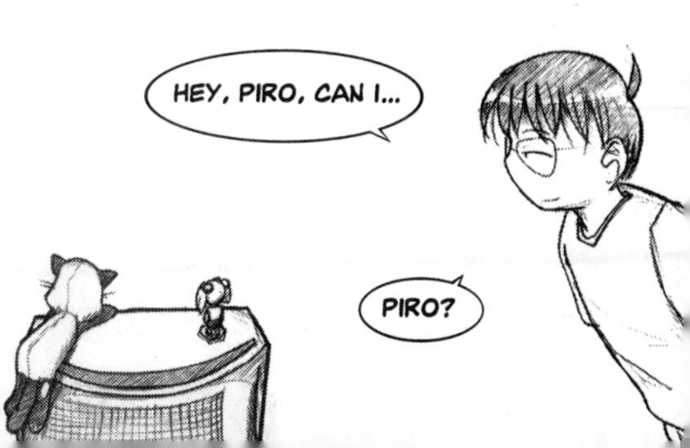
HEY, PIRO, CAN I...
PIRO?

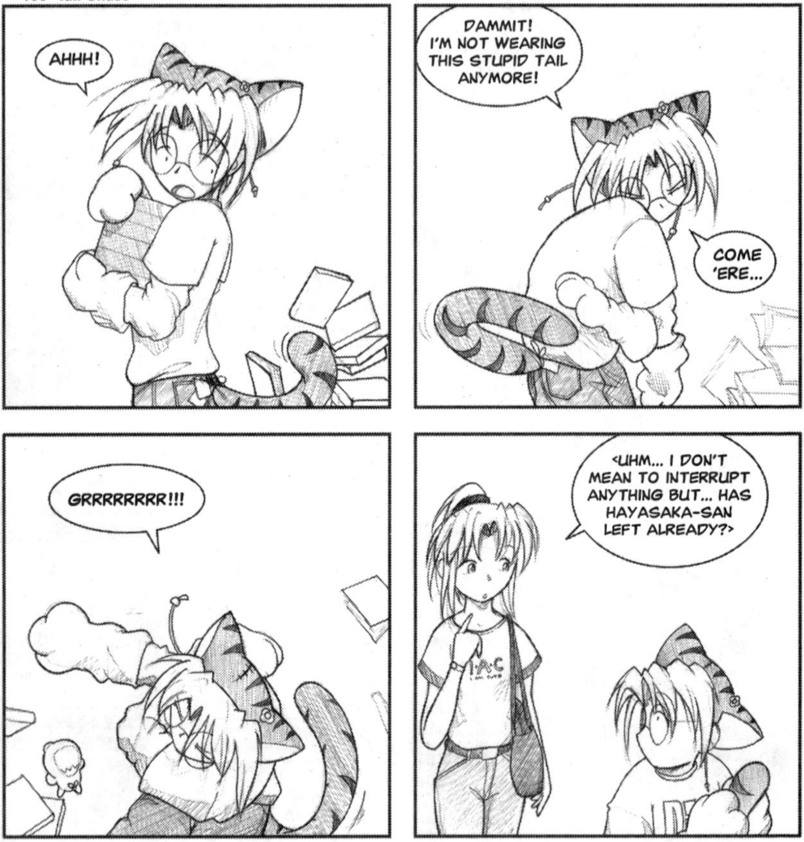
AHHH!
DAMMIT! I'M NOT WEARING THIS STUPID TAIL ANYMORE!
COME 'ERE...
GRRRRRRRR!!!
<UHM... I DON'T MEAN TO INTERRUPT ANYTHING BUT... HAS HAYASAKA-SAN LEFT ALREADY?>

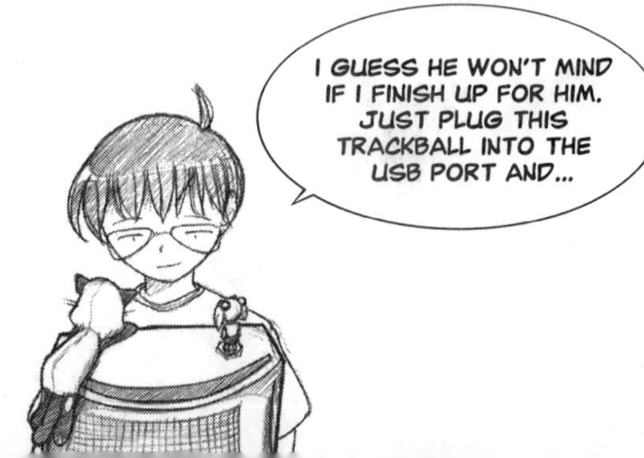
I GUESS HE WON'T MIND IF I FINISH UP FOR HIM. JUST PLUG THIS TRACKBALL INTO THE USB PORT AND...

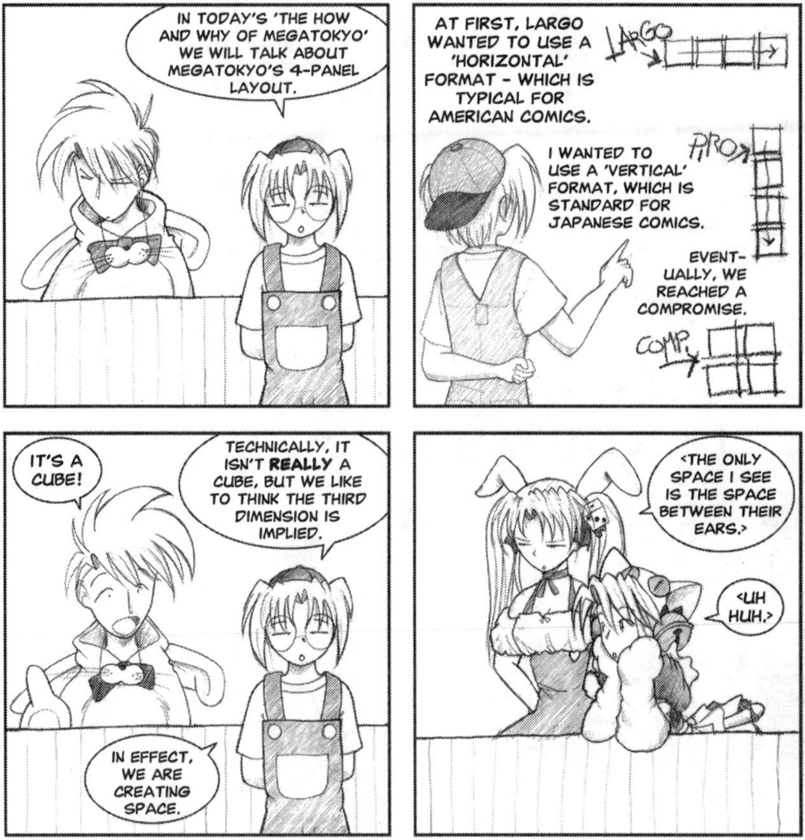
IN TODAY'S 'THE HOW AND WHY OF MEGATOKYO' WE WILL TALK ABOUT MEGATOKYO'S 4-PANEL LAYOUT.
AT FIRST, LARGO WANTED TO USE A 'HORIZONTAL' FORMAT - WHICH IS TYPICAL FOR AMERICAN COMICS.
LARGO
I WANTED TO USE A 'VERTICAL' FORMAT, WHICH IS STANDARD FOR JAPANESE COMICS.
PIRO
EVENT-UALLY, WE REACHED A COMPROMISE.
COMP.
IT'S A CUBE!
TECHNICALLY, IT ISN'T **REALLY** A CUBE, BUT WE LIKE TO THINK THE THIRD DIMENSION IS IMPLIED.
IN EFFECT, WE ARE CREATING SPACE.
<THE ONLY SPACE I SEE IS THE SPACE BETWEEN THEIR EARS.>
<UH HUH.>

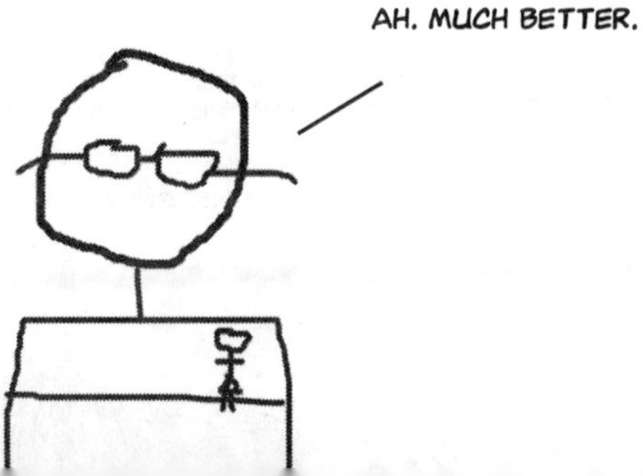
AH. MUCH BETTER.

WELCOME TO THIS SPECIAL SHIRT GUY DOM!
HERE, I GET TO MAKE FUN OF THE LAYOUT--
ESPECIALLY HOW WE SWITCHED LAYOUTS
JUST AS WE WERE GETTING USED
TO THE OLD FORMAT.

AND WHY? BECAUSE FRED
LIKES TO MAKE THINGS HARD
ON HIMSELF. NO MORE,
NO LESS.

THIS IS WHY I PUT IN THIS
PAGE--NO LAYOUT, NO PROBS!
IT'S ALSO MY ONLY CHANCE
TO SLIP IN SOME COMMENTS.
LIKE HOW WEIRD THE OLD
STUFF LOOKS... CHECK OUT
HOW THE FACES HAVE
CHANGED.

BUT DON'T FRET! THIS SECTION
IS PERFORATED SO THAT
YOU CAN BURN ALL THE OLD,
CRAPPY COMICS AND JUST
KEEP THE SLICK, HYPNOTICALLY
SHINY SGD COMICS!

(FIRE)

MT

(SPINE)

UMM, DOM... I THINK IT'S
PERFORATED SO PEOPLE CAN
THROW US AWAY.

SILENCE, PEASANT! LEST
I ERASE YOU WITH MY MIGHTY
POWERS OVER THIS GRAPHIC
NOVEL!

I'LL BE GOOD.

FOR A LIMITED ENGAGEMENT ONLY - SHIRT GUY DOM'S EMERGENCY STICK FIGURE ART DAY!

HEY, DOM HERE. SORRY THIS EPISODE LOOKS SO CRAPPY, BUT THERE'S NOTHING TO BE DONE.

(THESE ARE GLASSES)

SEE, PIRO IS STILL RECOVERING, AND HAS PERSONAL BUSINESS TO TAKE CARE OF.

(THERMOMETER)

MEANWHILE, LARGO HAS PERSONAL BUSINESS OF HIS OWN.

(THAT'S NOT PAC-MAN)

(BOOZE)

WHICH LEAVES IT UP TO ME TO DO SOMETHING FUNNY TODAY.

(BUNNY EARS)

(SWEAT DROPLET)

I WOULD PERSONALLY LIKE TO APOLOGIZE FOR TODAY'S STRIP. I HAVE TAKEN STEPS TO ENSURE THAT THIS WILL NEVER HAPPEN AGAIN.

IF YOU SEE DOM, TELL HIM THAT I KNOW WHERE HE LIVES, AND THAT HE CAN'T HIDE FROM ME FOREVER.

AH, THE EARLY DAYS OF MT. THE SAGA OF THE SHIRT GUY STARTS WITH LARGO, WHO GETS TIRED OF PEOPLE ASKING HIM ABOUT OUR NEWLY OPENED T-SHIRT STORE, AND SAYS "ALL QUESTIONS GO TO SHIRT GUY DOM." SO, I'M THE SHIRT GUY. I SHRUG IT OFF, SINCE IT DOESN'T MATTER TO ME.

THEN ONE NIGHT PIRO CAN'T FINISH THE COMIC ON TIME, AND I GET A MESSAGE FROM LARGO AROUND AN HOUR BEFORE WE'RE SCHEDULED TO UPDATE. "WE NEED THE SHIRT GUY TO DO STICK FIGURES," IT SAYS. I REALIZED THAT IT WOULD MAKE PEOPLE SUFFER, AND THE REST IS HISTORY. WE HAVEN'T BEEN SUED BY SLUGGY FREELANCE YET, SO I'D CONSIDER IT A SUCCESS.

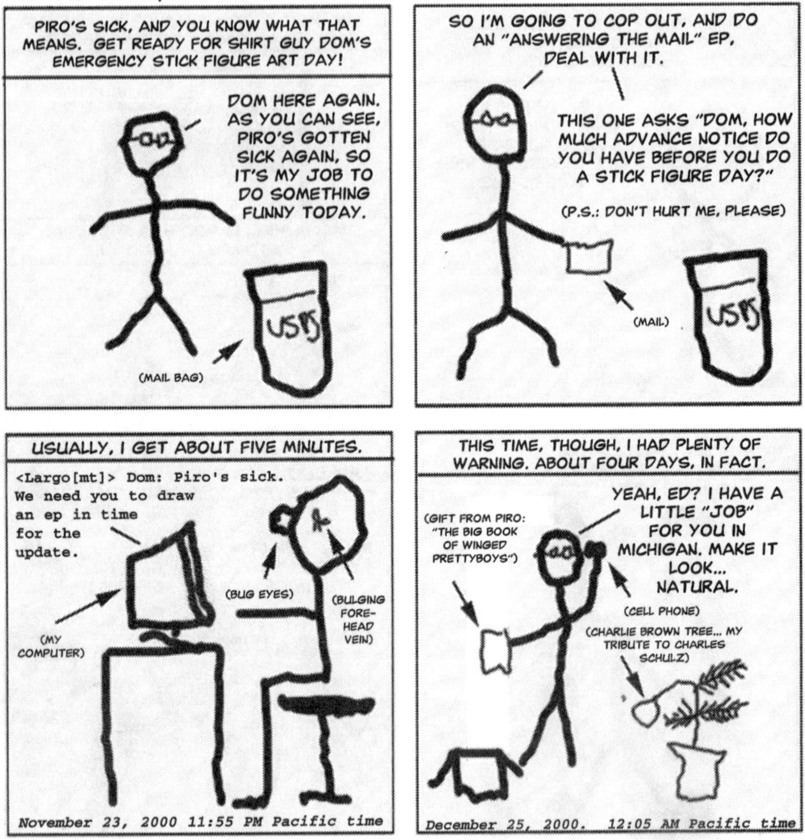
PIRO'S SICK, AND YOU KNOW WHAT THAT MEANS. GET READY FOR SHIRT GUY DOM'S EMERGENCY STICK FIGURE ART DAY!
DOM HERE AGAIN. AS YOU CAN SEE, PIRO'S GOTTEN SICK AGAIN, SO IT'S MY JOB TO DO SOMETHING FUNNY TODAY.
(MAIL BAG)
USPS
SO I'M GOING TO COP OUT, AND DO AN "ANSWERING THE MAIL" EP, DEAL WITH IT.
THIS ONE ASKS "DOM, HOW MUCH ADVANCE NOTICE DO YOU HAVE BEFORE YOU DO A STICK FIGURE DAY?"
(P.S.: DON'T HURT ME, PLEASE)
(MAIL)
USPS
USUALLY, I GET ABOUT FIVE MINUTES.
<Largo[mt]> Dom: Piro's sick. We need you to draw an ep in time for the update.
(MY COMPUTER)
(BUG EYES)
(BULGING FORE-HEAD VEIN)
November 23, 2000 11:55 PM Pacific time
THIS TIME, THOUGH, I HAD PLENTY OF WARNING. ABOUT FOUR DAYS, IN FACT.
(GIFT FROM PIRO: "THE BIG BOOK OF WINGED PRETTYBOYS")
YEAH, ED? I HAVE A LITTLE "JOB" FOR YOU IN MICHIGAN. MAKE IT LOOK... NATURAL.
(CELL PHONE)
(CHARLIE BROWN TREE... MY TRIBUTE TO CHARLES SCHULZ)
December 25, 2000. 12:05 AM Pacific time

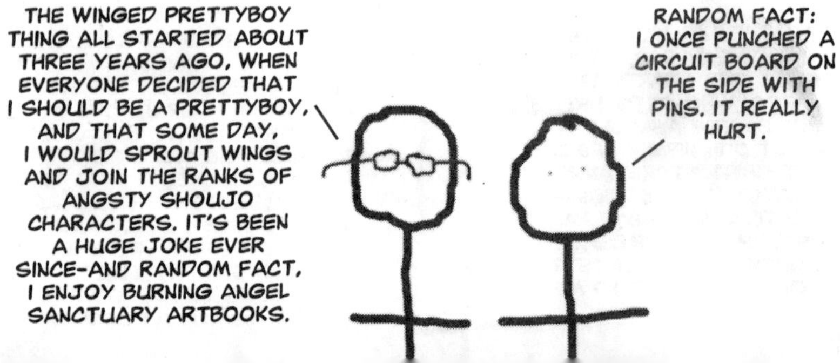
THE WINGED PRETTYBOY THING ALL STARTED ABOUT THREE YEARS AGO, WHEN EVERYONE DECIDED THAT I SHOULD BE A PRETTYBOY, AND THAT SOME DAY, I WOULD SPROUT WINGS AND JOIN THE RANKS OF ANGSTY SHOUJO CHARACTERS. IT'S BEEN A HUGE JOKE EVER SINCE-AND RANDOM FACT, I ENJOY BURNING ANGEL SANCTUARY ARTBOOKS.
RANDOM FACT: I ONCE PUNCHED A CIRCUIT BOARD ON THE SIDE WITH PINS. IT REALLY HURT.

BECAUSE I JUST CAN'T GET ENOUGH OF YOUR CRIES OF PAIN, HERE'S YET ANOTHER SHIRT GUY DOM STICK FIGURE ART DAY!

HERE WE GO AGAIN, BOYS AND GIRLS. PIRO HASN'T ANSWERED HIS PHONE OR HIS MAIL FOR A FEW DAYS, SO I GUESS IT'S MY TURN AGAIN.

DON'T WORRY, THIS STRIP WON'T BE JUST ME TALKING THIS TIME. ED'S PAYING A VISIT.

HEY, DOM! GLAD YOU CALLED, I JUST GOT BACK FROM THAT JOB IN MICHIGAN.

HEY, DO YOU KNOW WHAT HAPPENED TO PIRO? HE'S SUPPOSED TO BE DRAWING THE NEXT STRIP, BUT NO ONE CAN FIND HIM.

UH... WELL, I KNOW WHERE PART OF HIM IS, AT LEAST.

HMM? WHAT'S THAT SUPPOSED TO MEAN?

PROMISE YOU WON'T GET MAD?

HECK NO.

AAAAAH! YOU KILLED HIM? NOW WHAT ARE WE GONNA DO ABOUT THE NEXT STRIP?

DON'T WORRY, I CAN FIX HIM UP, GOOD AS NEW.

PIRO'S HEAD

JUST HOW ARE YOU PLANNING TO "FIX" A HEADLESS ARTIST?

JUST MASKING TAPE.

GOT ANY TAPE?

OKAY, NOW WE'RE JUST PLAIN SCREWED.

NOT GONNA HAPPEN

TRYING TO DRAW AN X WITH A TRACKBALL IS A WEIRD EXPERIENCE–I KEEP CHANGING HOW I DO DEAD EYES. IN THE EARLY ONES, I DREW IT, THEN I MOVED TO TYPING AN X WHERE THE EYES SHOULD BE, THEN I STARTED USING THE LINES. PHOTOSHOP IS A BLESSING, EVEN IF I ABUSE IT HORRIBLY.

RANDOM FACT: EARLY IN MT'S LIFE, LARGO WANTED TO INK THE COMICS. IT WAS QUICKLY DECIDED THAT THIS WAS NOT A FEASIBLE IDEA.

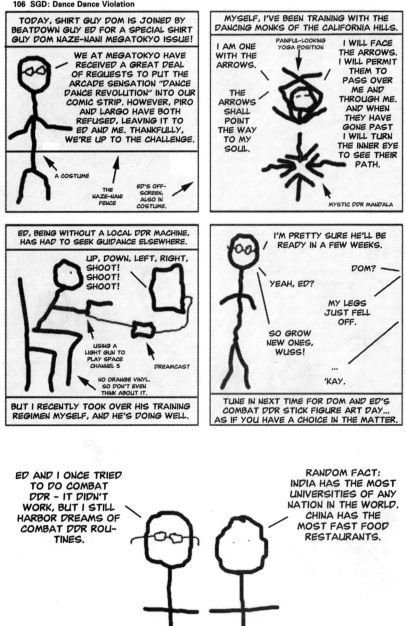

TODAY, SHIRT GUY DOM IS JOINED BY BEATDOWN GUY ED FOR A SPECIAL SHIRT GUY DOM NAZE-NANI MEGATOKYO ISSUE!

WE AT MEGATOKYO HAVE RECEIVED A GREAT DEAL OF REQUESTS TO PUT THE ARCADE SENSATION "DANCE DANCE REVOLUTION" INTO OUR COMIC STRIP. HOWEVER, PIRO AND LARGO HAVE BOTH REFUSED, LEAVING IT TO ED AND ME. THANKFULLY, WE'RE UP TO THE CHALLENGE.

A COSTUME

THE NAZE-NANI FENCE

ED'S OFF-SCREEN, ALSO IN COSTUME.

MYSELF, I'VE BEEN TRAINING WITH THE DANCING MONKS OF THE CALIFORNIA HILLS.

I AM ONE WITH THE ARROWS.

THE ARROWS SHALL POINT THE WAY TO MY SOUL.

PAINFUL-LOOKING YOGA POSITION

I WILL FACE THE ARROWS. I WILL PERMIT THEM TO PASS OVER ME AND THROUGH ME. AND WHEN THEY HAVE GONE PAST I WILL TURN THE INNER EYE TO SEE THEIR PATH.

MYSTIC DDR MANDALA

ED, BEING WITHOUT A LOCAL DDR MACHINE, HAS HAD TO SEEK GUIDANCE ELSEWHERE.

UP, DOWN, LEFT, RIGHT, SHOOT! SHOOT! SHOOT!

USING A LIGHT GUN TO PLAY SPACE CHANNEL 5

DREAMCAST

NO ORANGE VINYL, SO DON'T EVEN THINK ABOUT IT.

BUT I RECENTLY TOOK OVER HIS TRAINING REGIMEN MYSELF, AND HE'S DOING WELL.

I'M PRETTY SURE HE'LL BE READY IN A FEW WEEKS.

YEAH, ED?

DOM?

MY LEGS JUST FELL OFF.

SO GROW NEW ONES, WUSS!

...

'KAY.

TUNE IN NEXT TIME FOR DOM AND ED'S COMBAT DDR STICK FIGURE ART DAY... AS IF YOU HAVE A CHOICE IN THE MATTER.

ED AND I ONCE TRIED TO DO COMBAT DDR - IT DIDN'T WORK, BUT I STILL HARBOR DREAMS OF COMBAT DDR ROU-TINES.

RANDOM FACT: INDIA HAS THE MOST UNIVERSITIES OF ANY NATION IN THE WORLD. CHINA HAS THE MOST FAST FOOD RESTAURANTS.

PIRO'S TAKING A WELL-DESERVED DAY OFF, SO ONCE AGAIN IT'S TIME FOR DOM AND ED TO TAKE CENTER STAGE. DO YOU FEAR?

TODAY, WE'D LIKE TO SET ASIDE OUR USUAL HUMOR TO ADDRESS A SERIOUS MATTER-WORKER'S RIGHTS. SEE, PIRO AND LARGO GET ALL THE PERKS. HAIR, CLOTHES...

THEY GET EYES. WE GET... DOTS. WE DON'T EVEN GET MOUTHS!

THIS IS A DESK. USE YOUR IMAGINATION.

WE WON'T ASK FOR ALL THESE AT ONCE. WE HAVE ONE DEMAND: CONSCIENCES. BUT WE DON'T WANT ANY NAMBY-PAMBY FUZZY MASCOTS, NOR DO WE NEED TO PUMP OUR EGOS BY HAVING CUTE GIRLS SIT ON OUR SHOULDERS AND KIBITZ.

HEY, I DON'T SEE A PROBLEM WITH THAT LAST ONE...

THIS DEMAND MAY SEEM TRIFLING, BUT IT IS SIMPLY A STEP TOWARD COMIC EQUALITY.

YES, I HAVE LEGS BEHIND THIS THING, BUT YOU CAN'T SEE THEM, BECAUSE IT'S A DESK, STUPID.

SO, PIRO, THIS IS OUR REQUEST-NO, OUR CONDITION. GIVE US CONSCIENCES, PREFERABLY ONES THAT CAN CALL UP HELLFIRE, OR WE WALK.

THOSE RESPONSIBLE FOR THESE JOKES HAVE BEEN SACKED

CUT THE CRAP, DOM. LOOK, WE WANT IORI AND KYO ON OUR SHOULDERS. WE WANT THEM KICKING ASS, WE WANT THEM NOW, AND WE HAVE YOUR ADDRESS. YOU GOT THAT?

WE ARE A HEDGE.

AH, SORRY ABOUT THAT, FOLKS. I MAY BE BUSY, BUT I STILL HAVE LOTSA PACKING TAPE LEFT FROM MY MOVE.

THIS IS DOM.

HMGFF!

ER... I MAY HAVE USED A LITTLE TOO MUCH TAPE ON ED.

ED IS OVER HERE AND CAN'T EVEN MUMBLE →

THIS IS ANOTHER COSTUME I'VE ALWAYS WANTED TO DO. NO, NOT THE GAME CHARACTERS IN PANEL 3-BEEN THERE, DONE THAT. I WANT TO WANDER AROUND IN A BUNCH OF PACKING TAPE. IT'S NEVER HAPPENED, THOUGH, BECAUSE I HAPPEN TO LIKE BEING ABLE TO TALK AND BREATHE.

THE LAST FRAME LOOKS TERRIBLE BECAUSE PIRO LOST THE HIGH RES SCAN AND THE ORIGINAL DRAWING - THIS FRAME IS DIRECTLY FROM THE WEB VERSION. I THINK HE JUST TRIED TO MAKE IT GO AWAY.

RANDOM FACT: THE NBA INTRODUCED 24-SECOND SHOT CLOCK IN 1952.

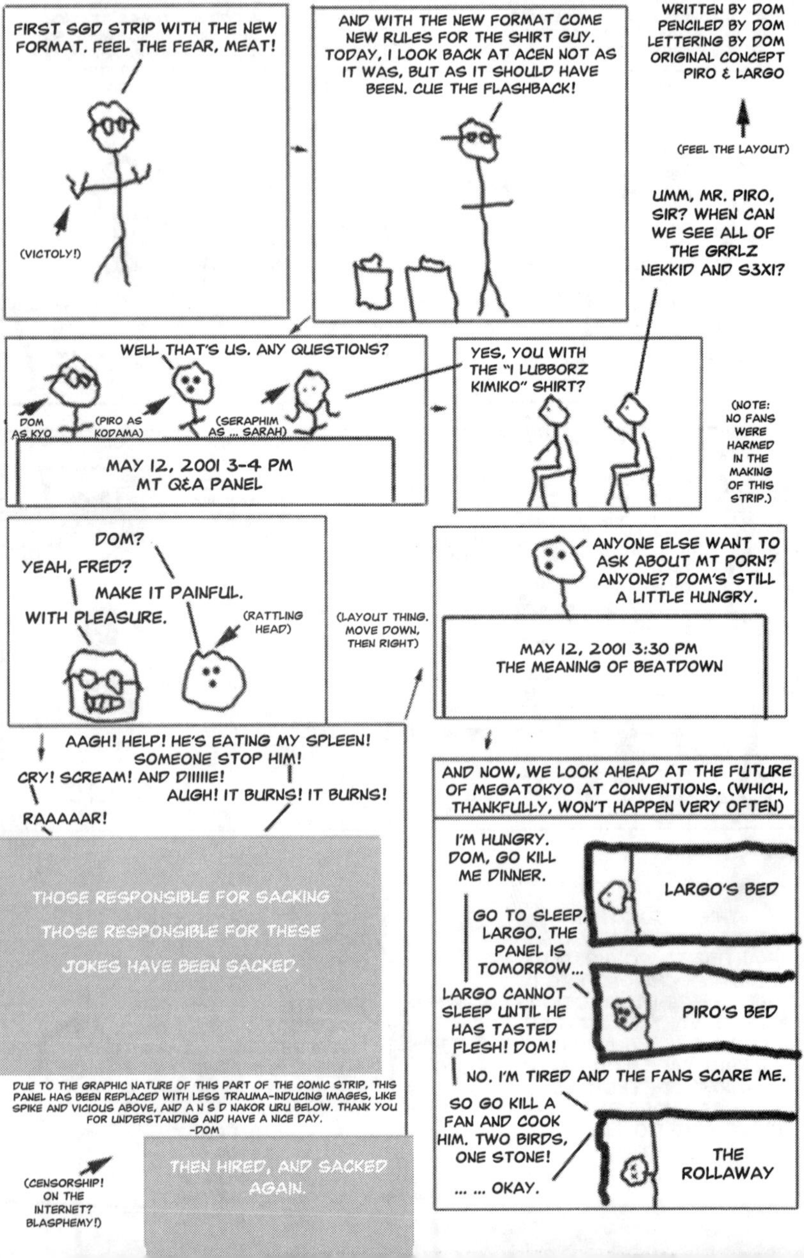
FIRST SGD STRIP WITH THE NEW FORMAT. FEEL THE FEAR, MEAT!
(VICTOLY!)
AND WITH THE NEW FORMAT COME NEW RULES FOR THE SHIRT GUY. TODAY, I LOOK BACK AT ACEN NOT AS IT WAS, BUT AS IT SHOULD HAVE BEEN. CUE THE FLASHBACK!
WRITTEN BY DOM
PENCILED BY DOM
LETTERING BY DOM
ORIGINAL CONCEPT
PIRO & LARGO
(FEEL THE LAYOUT)
WELL THAT'S US. ANY QUESTIONS?
DOM AS KYO
(PIRO AS KODAMA)
(SERAPHIM AS ... SARAH)
MAY 12, 2001 3-4 PM
MT Q&A PANEL
UMM, MR. PIRO, SIR? WHEN CAN WE SEE ALL OF THE GRRLZ NEKKID AND S3XI?
YES, YOU WITH THE "I LUBBORZ KIMIKO" SHIRT?
(NOTE: NO FANS WERE HARMED IN THE MAKING OF THIS STRIP.)
DOM?
YEAH, FRED?
MAKE IT PAINFUL.
WITH PLEASURE.
(RATTLING HEAD)
(LAYOUT THING. MOVE DOWN, THEN RIGHT)
ANYONE ELSE WANT TO ASK ABOUT MT PORN? ANYONE? DOM'S STILL A LITTLE HUNGRY.
MAY 12, 2001 3:30 PM
THE MEANING OF BEATDOWN
AAGH! HELP! HE'S EATING MY SPLEEN! SOMEONE STOP HIM!
CRY! SCREAM! AND DIIIIIE!
AUGH! IT BURNS! IT BURNS!
RAAAAAR!
THOSE RESPONSIBLE FOR SACKING THOSE RESPONSIBLE FOR THESE JOKES HAVE BEEN SACKED.
DUE TO THE GRAPHIC NATURE OF THIS PART OF THE COMIC STRIP, THIS PANEL HAS BEEN REPLACED WITH LESS TRAUMA-INDUCING IMAGES, LIKE SPIKE AND VICIOUS ABOVE, AND A N S D NAKOR URU BELOW. THANK YOU FOR UNDERSTANDING AND HAVE A NICE DAY.
-DOM
THEN HIRED, AND SACKED AGAIN.
(CENSORSHIP! ON THE INTERNET? BLASPHEMY!)
AND NOW, WE LOOK AHEAD AT THE FUTURE OF MEGATOKYO AT CONVENTIONS. (WHICH, THANKFULLY, WON'T HAPPEN VERY OFTEN)
I'M HUNGRY. DOM, GO KILL ME DINNER.
LARGO'S BED
GO TO SLEEP, LARGO. THE PANEL IS TOMORROW...
LARGO CANNOT SLEEP UNTIL HE HAS TASTED FLESH! DOM!
PIRO'S BED
NO. I'M TIRED AND THE FANS SCARE ME.
SO GO KILL A FAN AND COOK HIM. TWO BIRDS, ONE STONE!
... ... OKAY.
THE ROLLAWAY

OH NO!! ITS THE THE GIANT ERASER OF DOOM!! RUN!!

NOOOOOO OOOO!!!

SORRY ABOUT THAT.

AS I HAD MENTIONED EARLIER, I WAS STARTING TO FEEL CONSTRAINED BY THE FOUR PANEL FORMAT. WHEN WE STARTED MEGATOKYO, THE FORMAT WORKED GREAT BECAUSE IT SET REALISTIC BOUNDS ON WHAT I COULD DRAW IN A GIVEN EVENING.

AS THE STORY PROGRESSED, I REALIZED THAT THERE WERE THINGS THAT I JUST COULDN'T DO IN FOUR PANELS.

SINCE MY GOAL WAS TO ONE DAY DO A REAL MANGA, I DECIDED IT WAS TIME TO SWITCH TO A FULL PAGE FORMAT. MY DRAWING SPEED HAD INCREASED SO THAT THE COMIC WAS NO LONGER TAKING EIGHT HOURS TO PRODUCE. IT MADE SENSE, IN SOME SORT OF TWISTED, MASOCHISTIC WAY, THAT I COULD USE THAT EXTRA TIME TO DRAW MORE FOR EACH COMIC.

IT WAS ALSO AT THIS TIME THAT WE DECIDED TO START DIVIDING THINGS INTO CHAPTERS. EVERYTHING WE HAD DONE SO FAR WE CALLED "CHAPTER 0", AND ALL WE NEEDED TO DO WAS WRAP THINGS UP SO WE COULD START CHAPTER I AND START BEING A LITTLE MORE ORGANIZED.

YEAH, LIKE THAT COULD EVER HAPPEN. SO, WITHOUT FURTHER INTERRUPTION, I PRESENT THE LAST PART OF "CHAPTER 0" IN ITS FULL PAGE GLORY.

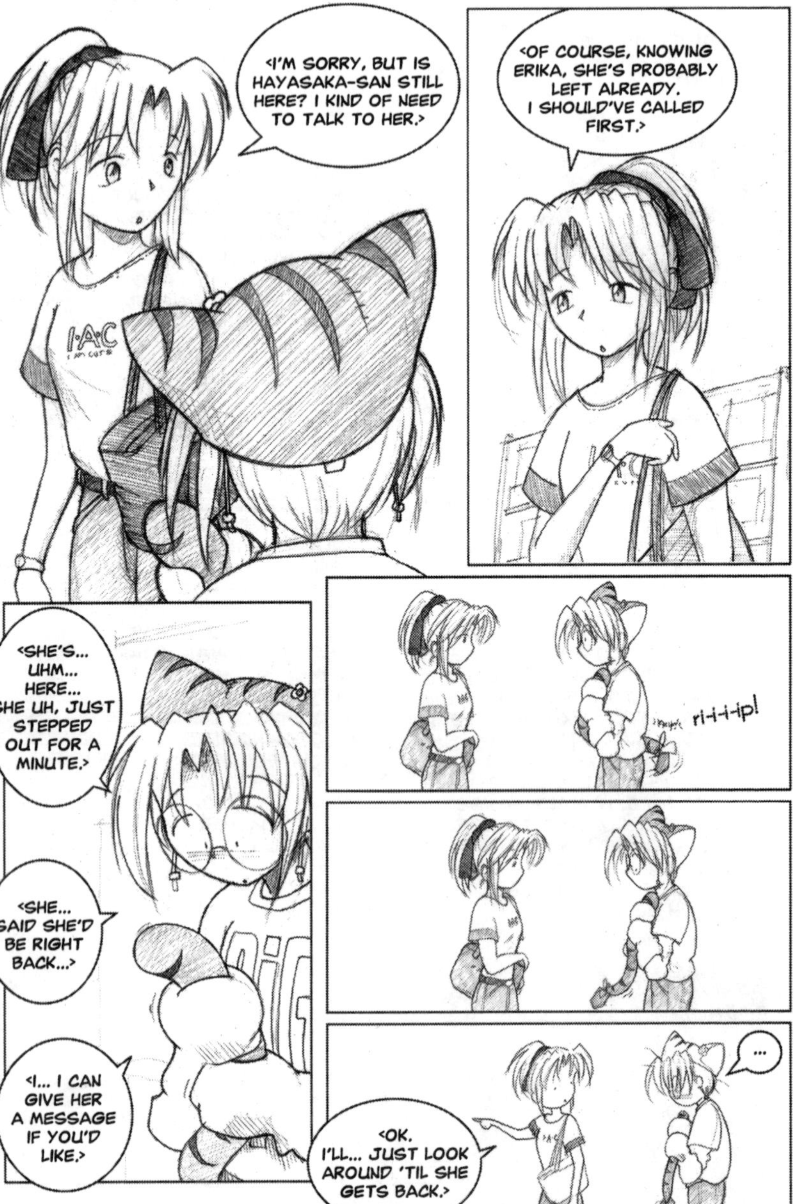
<I'M SORRY, BUT IS HAYASAKA-SAN STILL HERE? I KIND OF NEED TO TALK TO HER.>
<OF COURSE, KNOWING ERIKA, SHE'S PROBABLY LEFT ALREADY. I SHOULD'VE CALLED FIRST.>
<SHE'S... UHM... HERE... SHE UH, JUST STEPPED OUT FOR A MINUTE.>
<SHE... SAID SHE'D BE RIGHT BACK...>
<I... I CAN GIVE HER A MESSAGE IF YOU'D LIKE.>
ri-i-i-ip!
...
<OK. I'LL... JUST LOOK AROUND 'TIL SHE GETS BACK.>

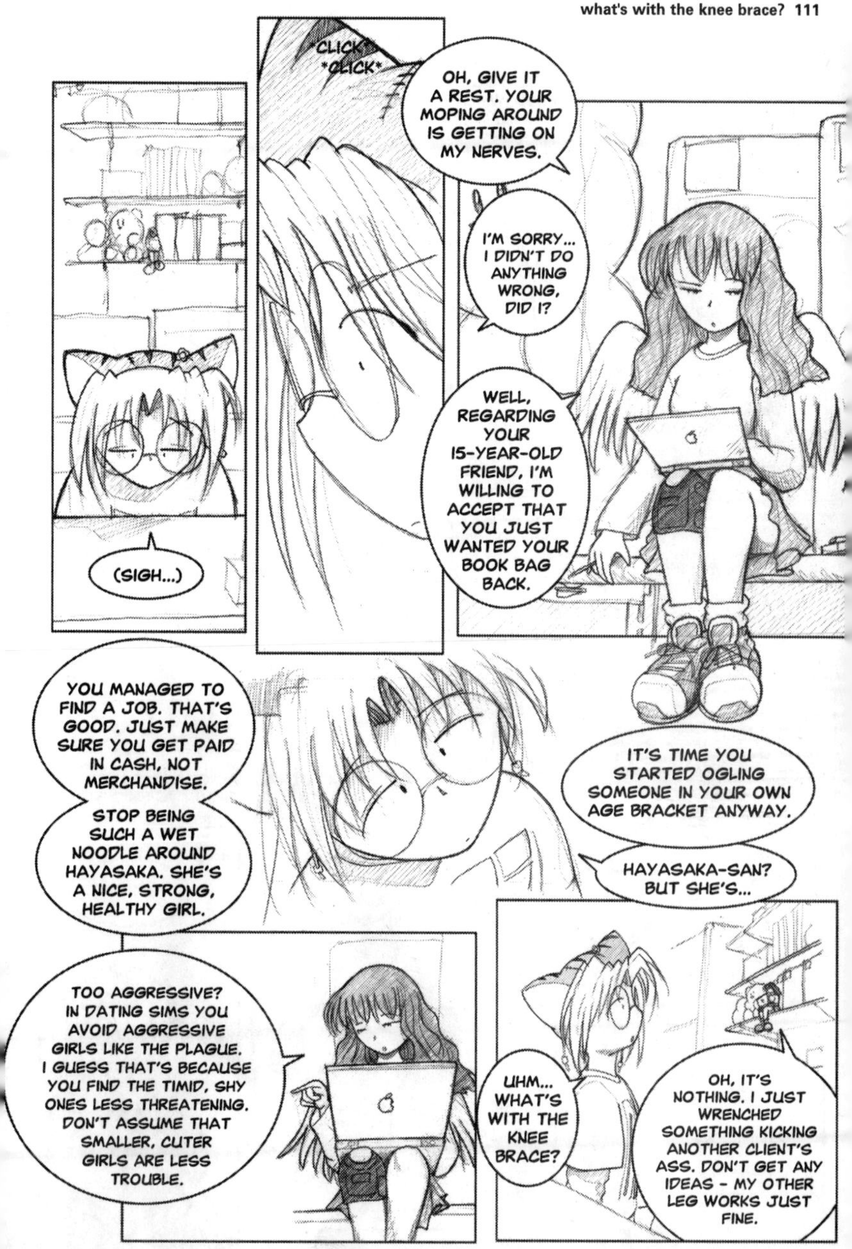
(SIGH...)
CLICK
CLICK
OH, GIVE IT A REST. YOUR MOPING AROUND IS GETTING ON MY NERVES.
I'M SORRY... I DIDN'T DO ANYTHING WRONG, DID I?
WELL, REGARDING YOUR 15-YEAR-OLD FRIEND, I'M WILLING TO ACCEPT THAT YOU JUST WANTED YOUR BOOK BAG BACK.
YOU MANAGED TO FIND A JOB. THAT'S GOOD. JUST MAKE SURE YOU GET PAID IN CASH, NOT MERCHANDISE.
STOP BEING SUCH A WET NOODLE AROUND HAYASAKA. SHE'S A NICE, STRONG, HEALTHY GIRL.
IT'S TIME YOU STARTED OGLING SOMEONE IN YOUR OWN AGE BRACKET ANYWAY.
HAYASAKA-SAN? BUT SHE'S...
TOO AGGRESSIVE? IN DATING SIMS YOU AVOID AGGRESSIVE GIRLS LIKE THE PLAGUE. I GUESS THAT'S BECAUSE YOU FIND THE TIMID, SHY ONES LESS THREATENING. DON'T ASSUME THAT SMALLER, CUTER GIRLS ARE LESS TROUBLE.
UHM... WHAT'S WITH THE KNEE BRACE?
OH, IT'S NOTHING. I JUST WRENCHED SOMETHING KICKING ANOTHER CLIENT'S ASS. DON'T GET ANY IDEAS - MY OTHER LEG WORKS JUST FINE.

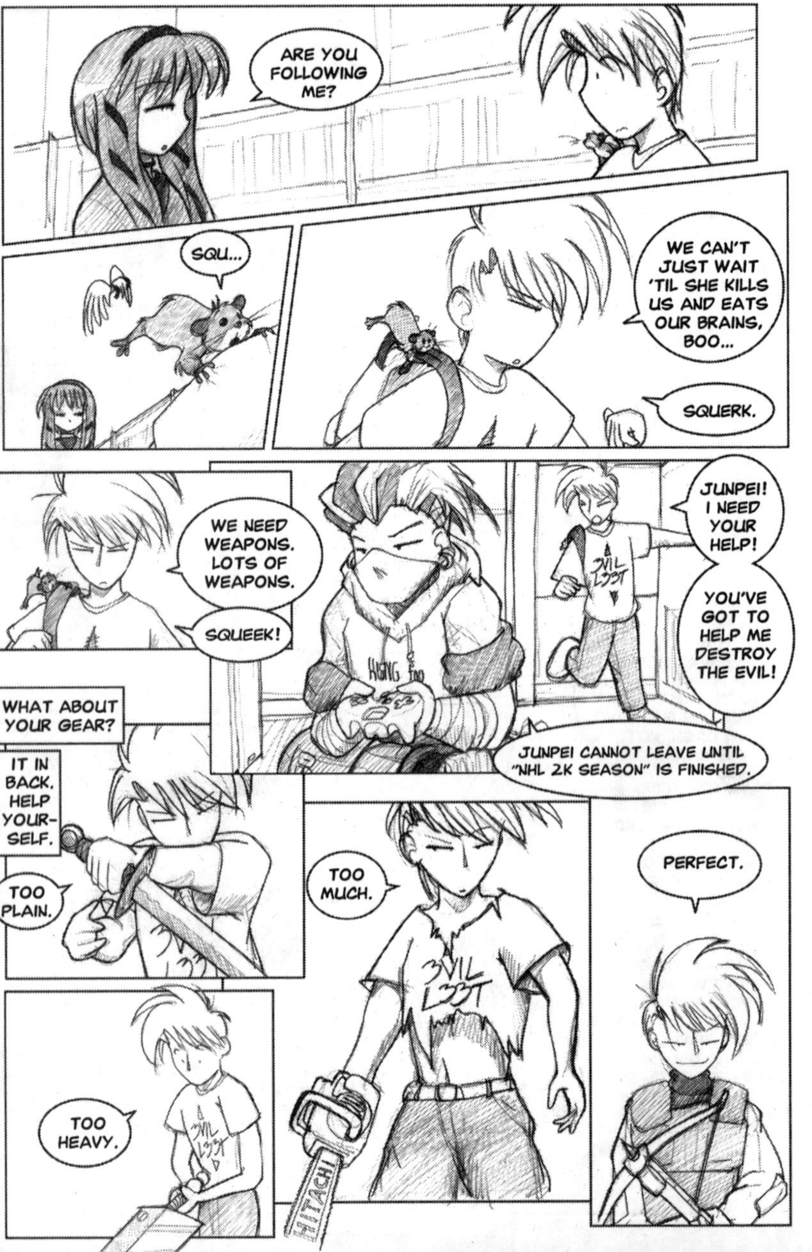
ARE YOU FOLLOWING ME?
SQU...
WE CAN'T JUST WAIT 'TIL SHE KILLS US AND EATS OUR BRAINS, BOO...
SQUERK.
WE NEED WEAPONS. LOTS OF WEAPONS.
SQUEEK!
JUNPEI! I NEED YOUR HELP!
YOU'VE GOT TO HELP ME DESTROY THE EVIL!
JUNPEI CANNOT LEAVE UNTIL "NHL 2K SEASON" IS FINISHED.
WHAT ABOUT YOUR GEAR?
IT IN BACK. HELP YOUR-SELF.
TOO PLAIN.
TOO HEAVY.
TOO MUCH.
PERFECT.

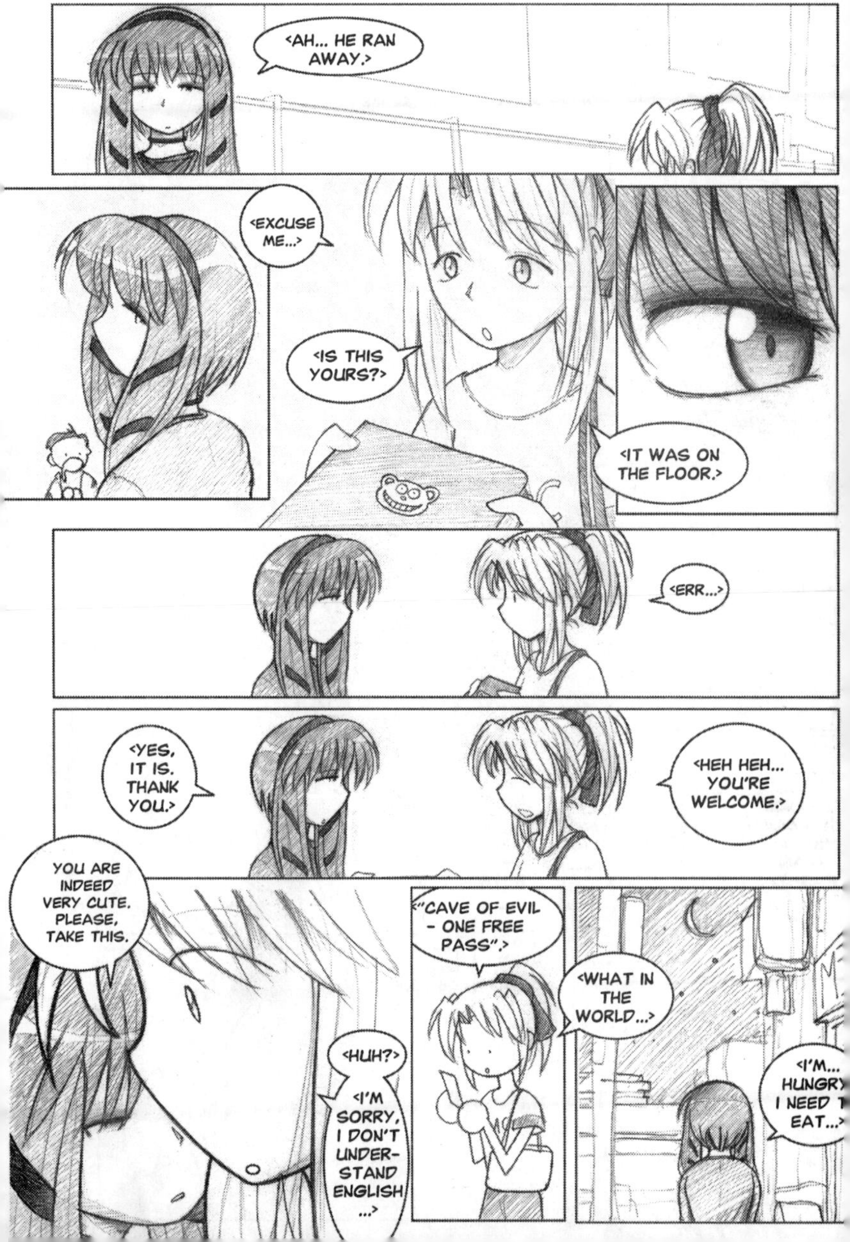
<AH... HE RAN AWAY.>
<EXCUSE ME...>
<IS THIS YOURS?>
<IT WAS ON THE FLOOR.>
<ERR...>
<YES, IT IS. THANK YOU.>
<HEH HEH... YOU'RE WELCOME.>
YOU ARE INDEED VERY CUTE. PLEASE, TAKE THIS.
<HUH?>
<I'M SORRY, I DON'T UNDER-STAND ENGLISH ...>
<"CAVE OF EVIL - ONE FREE PASS".>
<WHAT IN THE WORLD...>
<I'M... HUNGRY I NEED T EAT...>

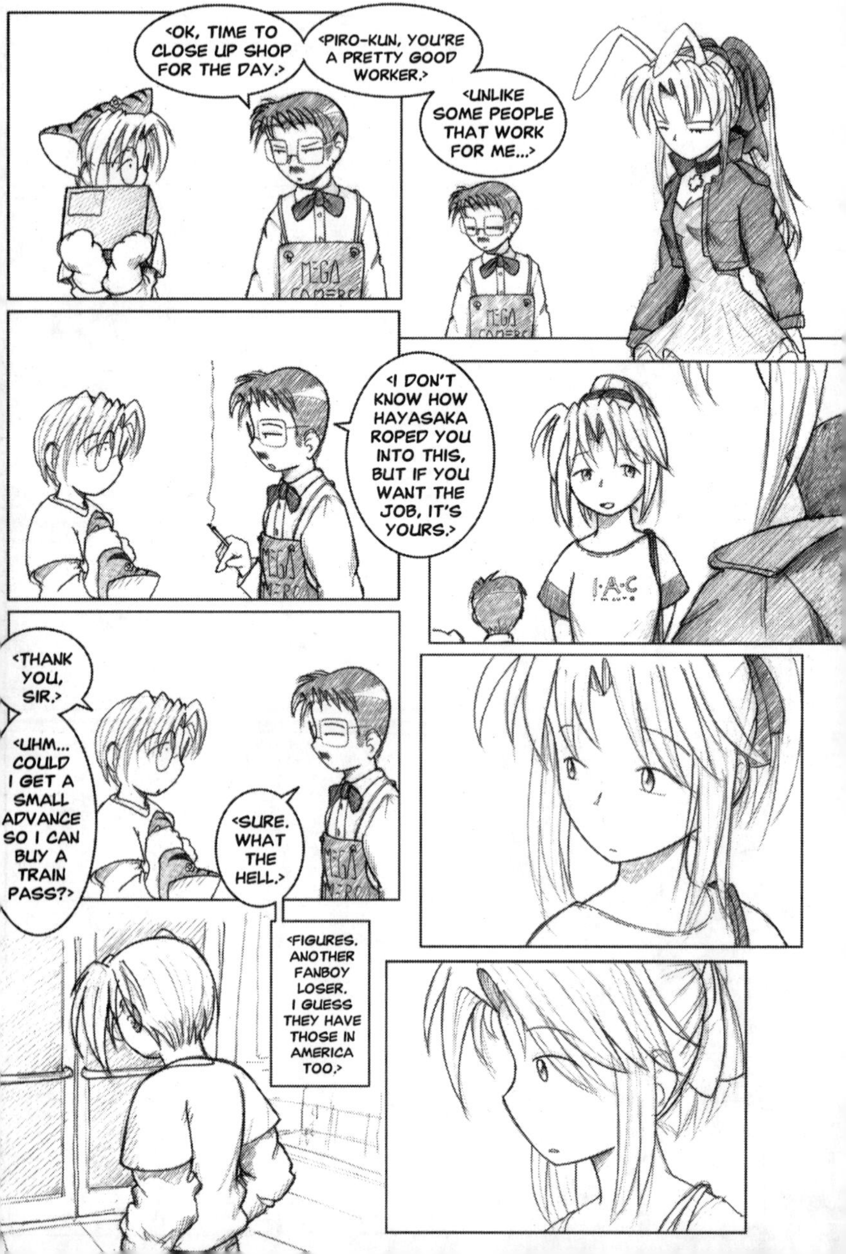

<OK, TIME TO CLOSE UP SHOP FOR THE DAY.>
<PIRO-KUN, YOU'RE A PRETTY GOOD WORKER.>
<UNLIKE SOME PEOPLE THAT WORK FOR ME...>
MEGA GAMERS
<I DON'T KNOW HOW HAYASAKA ROPED YOU INTO THIS, BUT IF YOU WANT THE JOB, IT'S YOURS.>
I·A·C
<THANK YOU, SIR.>
<UHM... COULD I GET A SMALL ADVANCE SO I CAN BUY A TRAIN PASS?>
<SURE. WHAT THE HELL.>
<FIGURES. ANOTHER FANBOY LOSER. I GUESS THEY HAVE THOSE IN AMERICA TOO.>

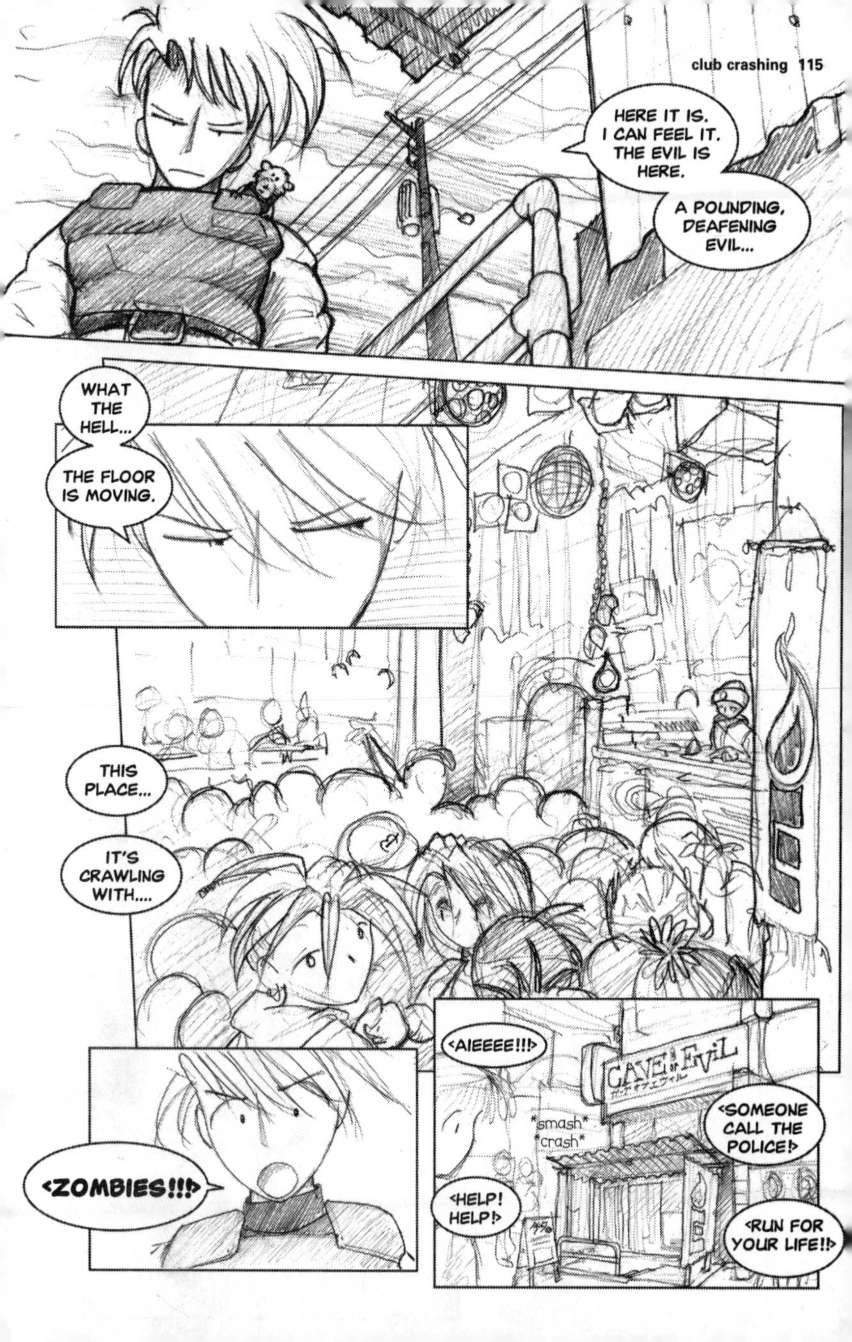
HERE IT IS. I CAN FEEL IT. THE EVIL IS HERE.
A POUNDING, DEAFENING EVIL...
WHAT THE HELL...
THE FLOOR IS MOVING.
THIS PLACE...
IT'S CRAWLING WITH....
<ZOMBIES!!!>
<AIEEEE!!!>
CAVE OF EVIL
smash
crash
<SOMEONE CALL THE POLICE!>
<HELP! HELP!>
<RUN FOR YOUR LIFE!!>

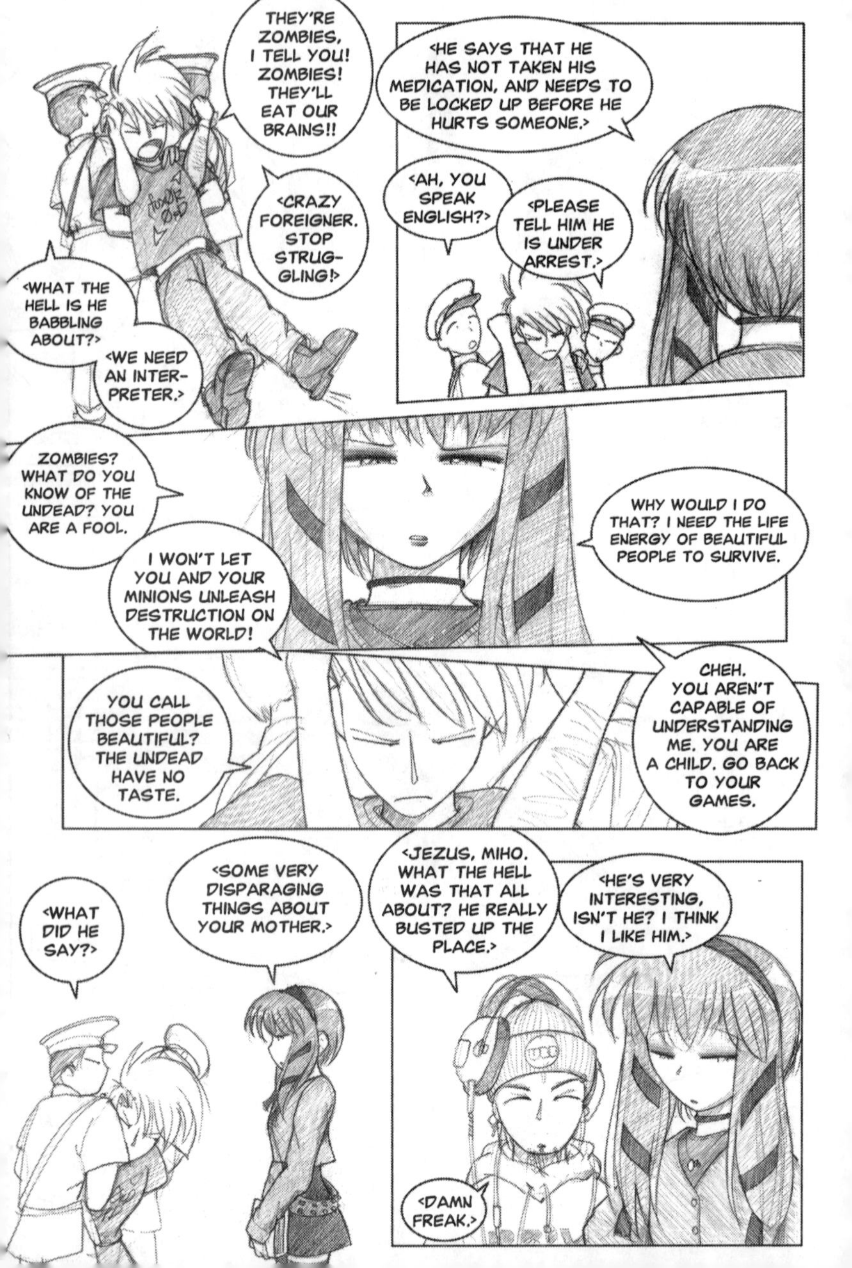
THEY'RE ZOMBIES, I TELL YOU! ZOMBIES! THEY'LL EAT OUR BRAINS!!
<CRAZY FOREIGNER. STOP STRUG-GLING!>
<WHAT THE HELL IS HE BABBLING ABOUT?>
<WE NEED AN INTER-PRETER.>
<HE SAYS THAT HE HAS NOT TAKEN HIS MEDICATION, AND NEEDS TO BE LOCKED UP BEFORE HE HURTS SOMEONE.>
<AH, YOU SPEAK ENGLISH?>
<PLEASE TELL HIM HE IS UNDER ARREST.>
ZOMBIES? WHAT DO YOU KNOW OF THE UNDEAD? YOU ARE A FOOL.
I WON'T LET YOU AND YOUR MINIONS UNLEASH DESTRUCTION ON THE WORLD!
WHY WOULD I DO THAT? I NEED THE LIFE ENERGY OF BEAUTIFUL PEOPLE TO SURVIVE.
YOU CALL THOSE PEOPLE BEAUTIFUL? THE UNDEAD HAVE NO TASTE.
CHEH. YOU AREN'T CAPABLE OF UNDERSTANDING ME. YOU ARE A CHILD. GO BACK TO YOUR GAMES.
<WHAT DID HE SAY?>
<SOME VERY DISPARAGING THINGS ABOUT YOUR MOTHER.>
<JEZUS, MIHO. WHAT THE HELL WAS THAT ALL ABOUT? HE REALLY BUSTED UP THE PLACE.>
<HE'S VERY INTERESTING, ISN'T HE? I THINK I LIKE HIM.>
<DAMN FREAK.>

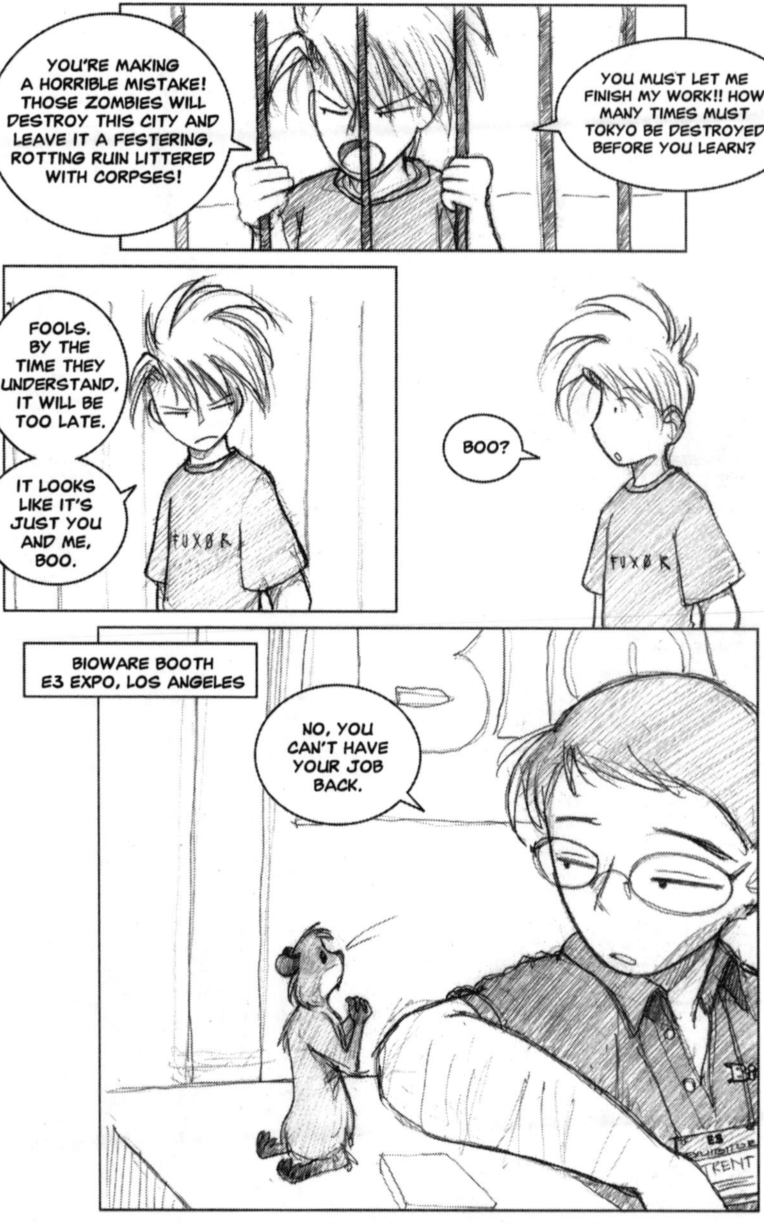
YOU'RE MAKING A HORRIBLE MISTAKE! THOSE ZOMBIES WILL DESTROY THIS CITY AND LEAVE IT A FESTERING, ROTTING RUIN LITTERED WITH CORPSES!
YOU MUST LET ME FINISH MY WORK!! HOW MANY TIMES MUST TOKYO BE DESTROYED BEFORE YOU LEARN?
FOOLS. BY THE TIME THEY UNDERSTAND, IT WILL BE TOO LATE.
IT LOOKS LIKE IT'S JUST YOU AND ME, BOO.
BOO?
BIOWARE BOOTH
E3 EXPO, LOS ANGELES
NO, YOU CAN'T HAVE YOUR JOB BACK.

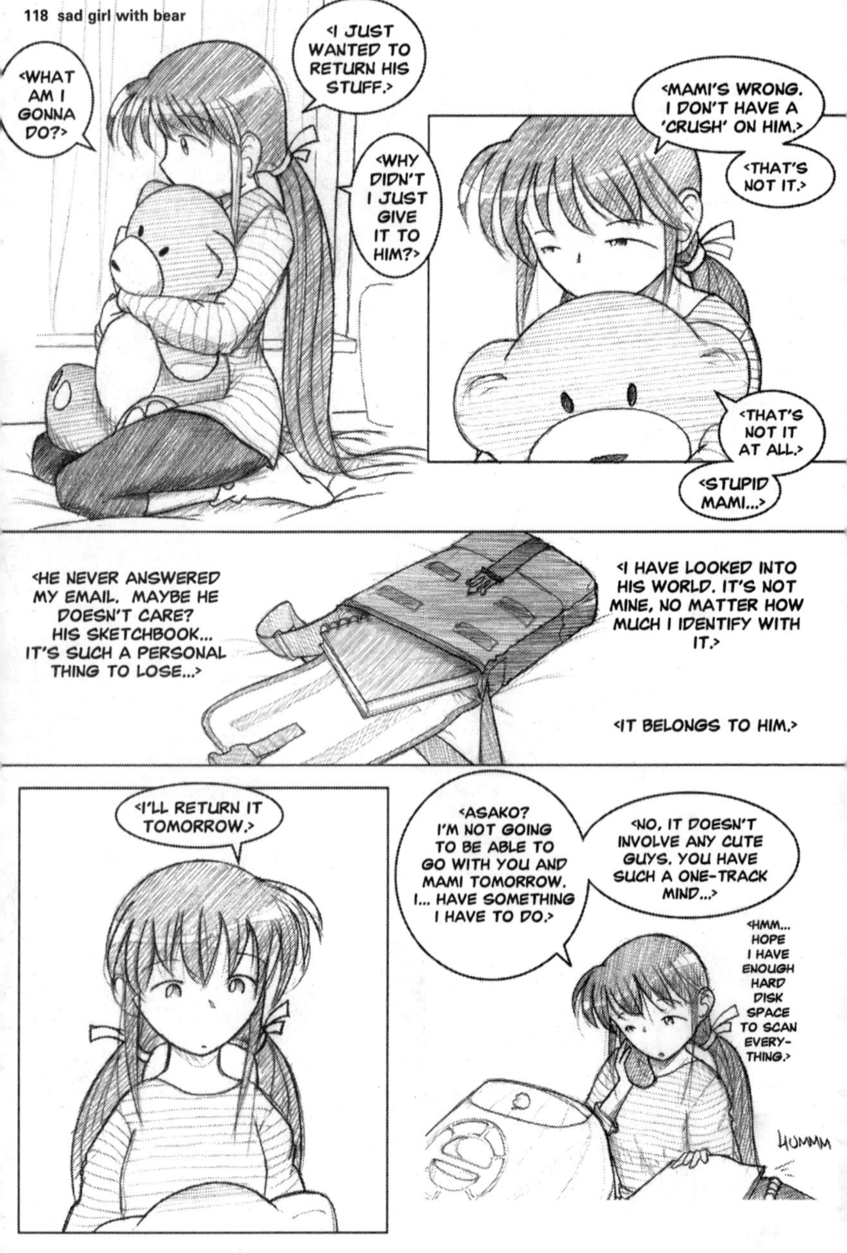
<WHAT AM I GONNA DO?>
<I JUST WANTED TO RETURN HIS STUFF.>
<WHY DIDN'T I JUST GIVE IT TO HIM?>
<MAMI'S WRONG. I DON'T HAVE A 'CRUSH' ON HIM.>
<THAT'S NOT IT.>
<THAT'S NOT IT AT ALL.>
<STUPID MAMI...>
<HE NEVER ANSWERED MY EMAIL. MAYBE HE DOESN'T CARE? HIS SKETCHBOOK... IT'S SUCH A PERSONAL THING TO LOSE...>
<I HAVE LOOKED INTO HIS WORLD. IT'S NOT MINE, NO MATTER HOW MUCH I IDENTIFY WITH IT.>
<IT BELONGS TO HIM.>
<I'LL RETURN IT TOMORROW.>
<ASAKO? I'M NOT GOING TO BE ABLE TO GO WITH YOU AND MAMI TOMORROW. I... HAVE SOMETHING I HAVE TO DO.>
<NO, IT DOESN'T INVOLVE ANY CUTE GUYS. YOU HAVE SUCH A ONE-TRACK MIND...>
<HMM... HOPE I HAVE ENOUGH HARD DISK SPACE TO SCAN EVERYTHING.>
HUMMM

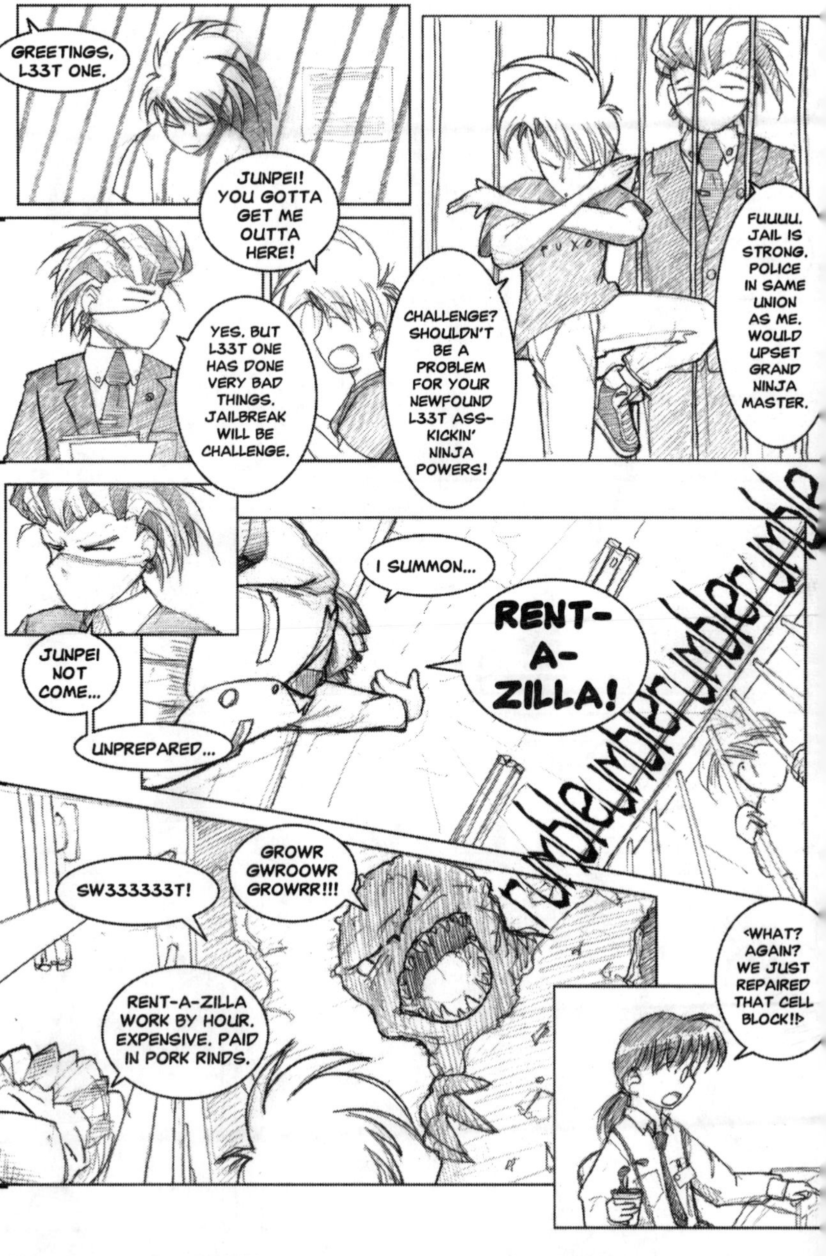
GREETINGS, L33T ONE.
JUNPEI! YOU GOTTA GET ME OUTTA HERE!
YES. BUT L33T ONE HAS DONE VERY BAD THINGS. JAILBREAK WILL BE CHALLENGE.
CHALLENGE? SHOULDN'T BE A PROBLEM FOR YOUR NEWFOUND L33T ASS-KICKIN' NINJA POWERS!
FUUUU. JAIL IS STRONG. POLICE IN SAME UNION AS ME. WOULD UPSET GRAND NINJA MASTER.
JUNPEI NOT COME...
UNPREPARED...
I SUMMON...
RENT-A-ZILLA!
SW333333T!
GROWR GWROOWR GROWRR!!!
RENT-A-ZILLA WORK BY HOUR. EXPENSIVE. PAID IN PORK RINDS.
<WHAT? AGAIN? WE JUST REPAIRED THAT CELL BLOCK!!>

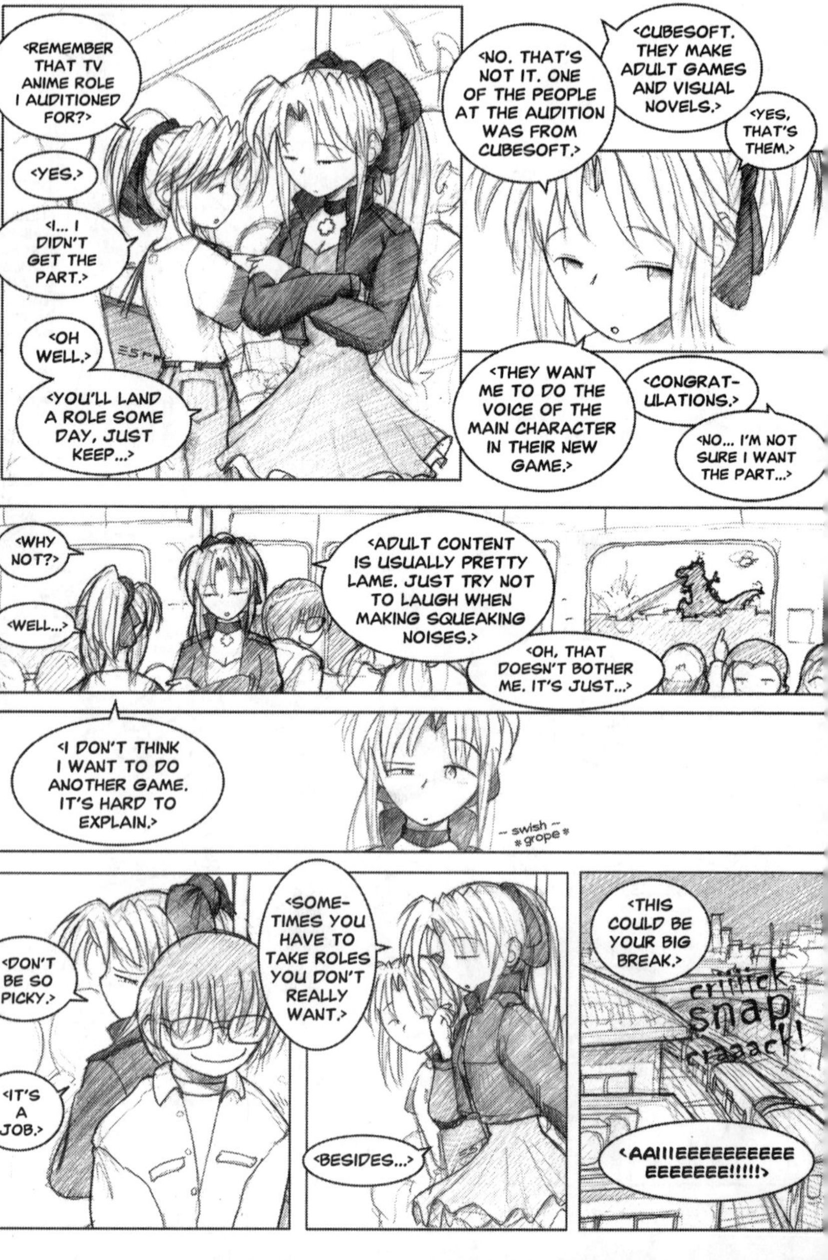
<REMEMBER THAT TV ANIME ROLE I AUDITIONED FOR?>
<YES.>
<I... I DIDN'T GET THE PART.>
<OH WELL.>
<YOU'LL LAND A ROLE SOME DAY, JUST KEEP...>
<NO. THAT'S NOT IT. ONE OF THE PEOPLE AT THE AUDITION WAS FROM CUBESOFT.>
<CUBESOFT. THEY MAKE ADULT GAMES AND VISUAL NOVELS.>
<YES, THAT'S THEM.>
<THEY WANT ME TO DO THE VOICE OF THE MAIN CHARACTER IN THEIR NEW GAME.>
<CONGRAT-ULATIONS.>
<NO... I'M NOT SURE I WANT THE PART...>
<WHY NOT?>
<WELL...>
<ADULT CONTENT IS USUALLY PRETTY LAME. JUST TRY NOT TO LAUGH WHEN MAKING SQUEAKING NOISES.>
<OH, THAT DOESN'T BOTHER ME. IT'S JUST...>
<I DON'T THINK I WANT TO DO ANOTHER GAME. IT'S HARD TO EXPLAIN.>
~ swish ~
* grope *
<DON'T BE SO PICKY.>
<IT'S A JOB.>
<SOME-TIMES YOU HAVE TO TAKE ROLES YOU DON'T REALLY WANT.>
<BESIDES...>
<THIS COULD BE YOUR BIG BREAK.>
criiick
snap
craaack!
<AAIIIEEEEEEEEEEEEEEEEE!!!!!>

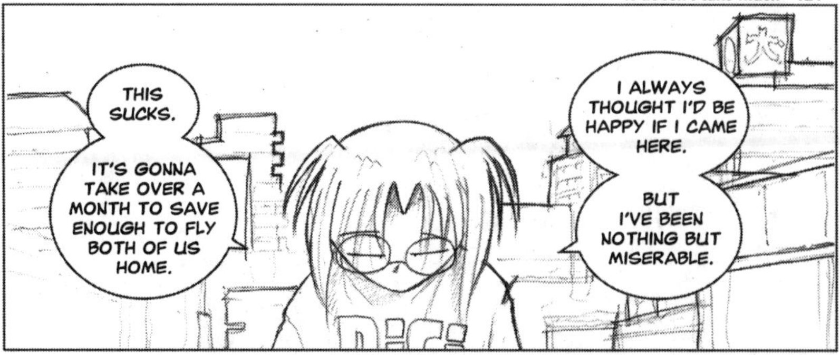
THIS SUCKS.
IT'S GONNA TAKE OVER A MONTH TO SAVE ENOUGH TO FLY BOTH OF US HOME.
I ALWAYS THOUGHT I'D BE HAPPY IF I CAME HERE.
BUT I'VE BEEN NOTHING BUT MISERABLE.

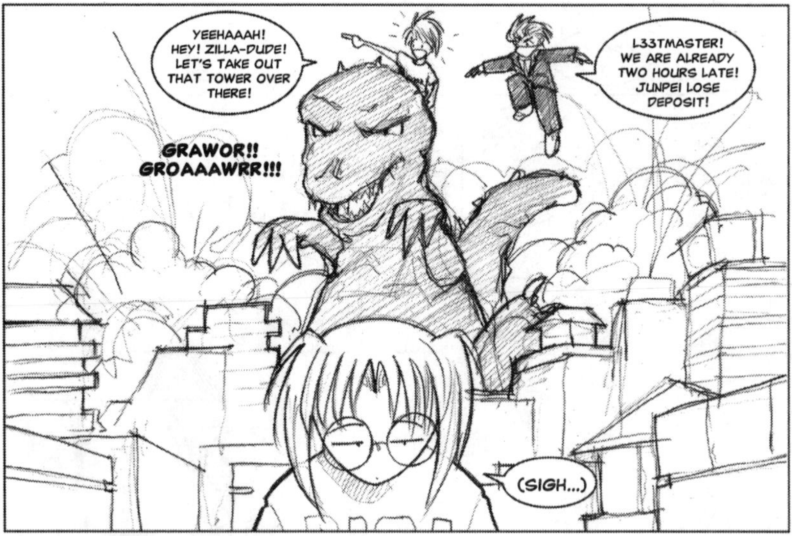
YEEHAAAH! HEY! ZILLA-DUDE! LET'S TAKE OUT THAT TOWER OVER THERE!
L33TMASTER! WE ARE ALREADY TWO HOURS LATE! JUNPEI LOSE DEPOSIT!
GRAWOR!! GROAAAWRR!!!
(SIGH...)

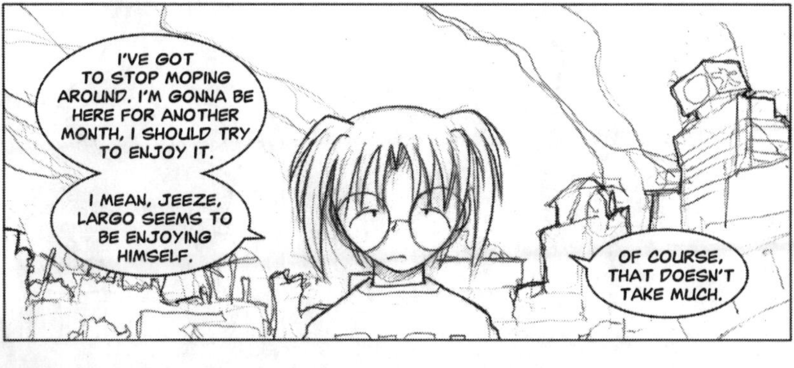
I'VE GOT TO STOP MOPING AROUND. I'M GONNA BE HERE FOR ANOTHER MONTH, I SHOULD TRY TO ENJOY IT.
I MEAN, JEEZE, LARGO SEEMS TO BE ENJOYING HIMSELF.
OF COURSE, THAT DOESN'T TAKE MUCH.

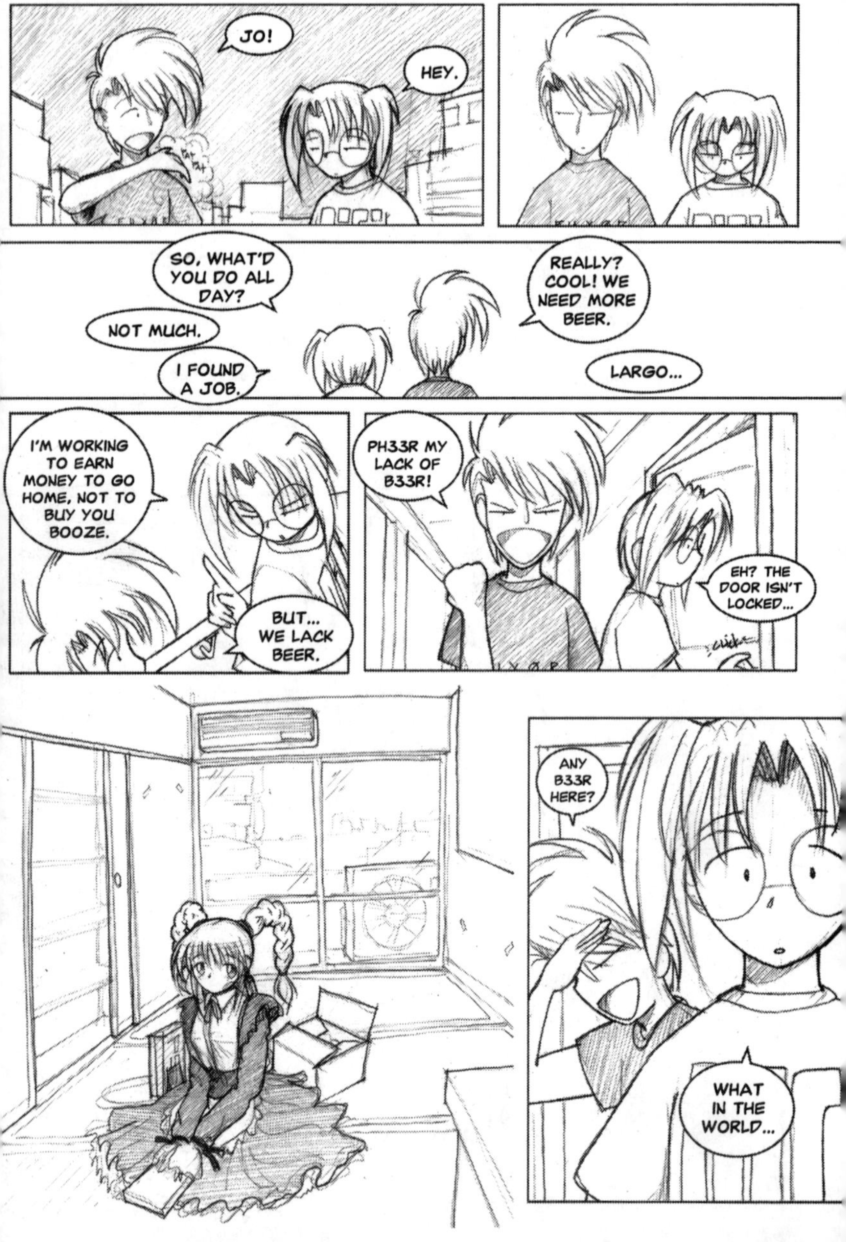
JO!
HEY.
SO, WHAT'D YOU DO ALL DAY?
NOT MUCH.
I FOUND A JOB.
REALLY? COOL! WE NEED MORE BEER.
LARGO...
I'M WORKING TO EARN MONEY TO GO HOME, NOT TO BUY YOU BOOZE.
BUT... WE LACK BEER.
PH33R MY LACK OF B33R!
EH? THE DOOR ISN'T LOCKED...
ANY B33R HERE?
WHAT IN THE WORLD...

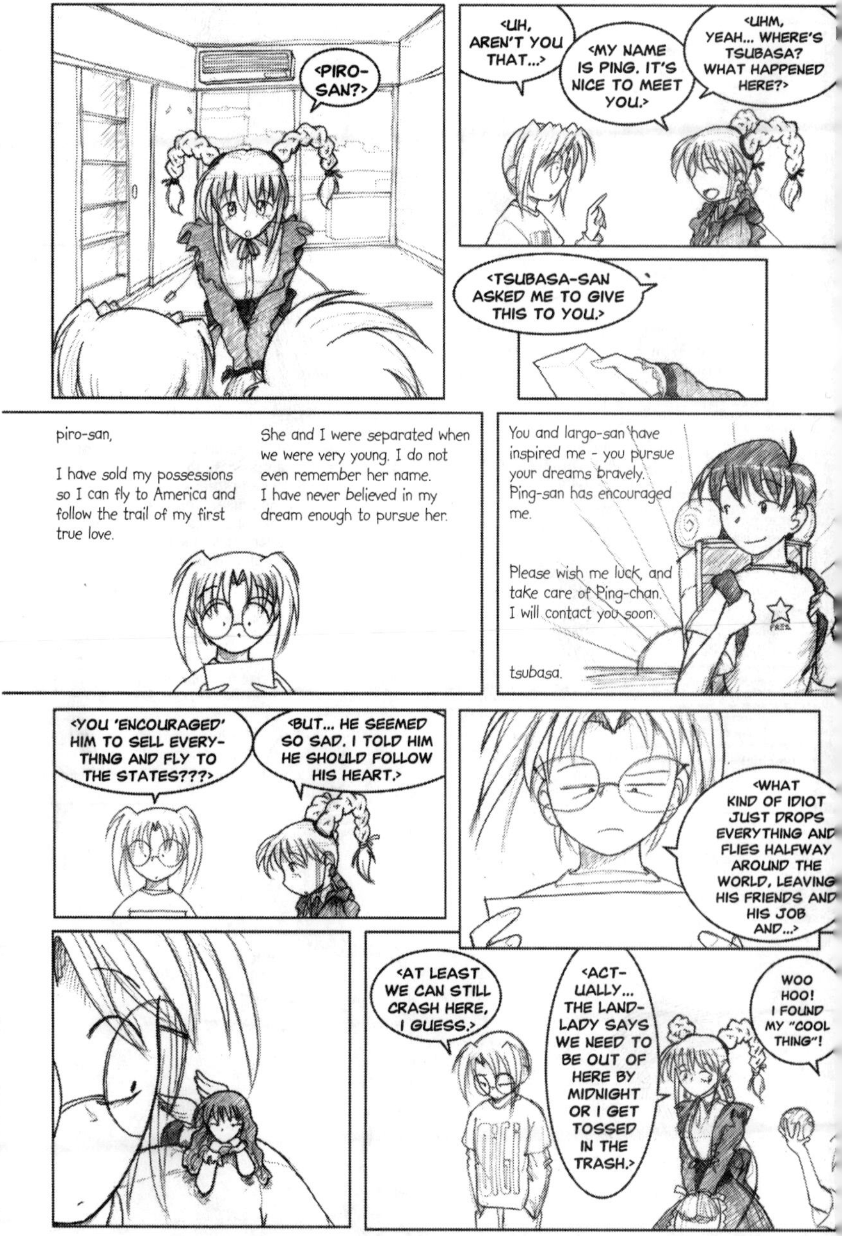

<PIRO-SAN?>
<UH, AREN'T YOU THAT...>
<MY NAME IS PING. IT'S NICE TO MEET YOU.>
<UHM, YEAH... WHERE'S TSUBASA? WHAT HAPPENED HERE?>
<TSUBASA-SAN ASKED ME TO GIVE THIS TO YOU.>
piro-san,
I have sold my possessions so I can fly to America and follow the trail of my first true love.
She and I were separated when we were very young. I do not even remember her name. I have never believed in my dream enough to pursue her.
You and largo-san have inspired me - you pursue your dreams bravely. Ping-san has encouraged me.
Please wish me luck, and take care of Ping-chan. I will contact you soon.
tsubasa.
<YOU 'ENCOURAGED' HIM TO SELL EVERYTHING AND FLY TO THE STATES???>
<BUT... HE SEEMED SO SAD. I TOLD HIM HE SHOULD FOLLOW HIS HEART.>
<WHAT KIND OF IDIOT JUST DROPS EVERYTHING AND FLIES HALFWAY AROUND THE WORLD, LEAVING HIS FRIENDS AND HIS JOB AND...>
<AT LEAST WE CAN STILL CRASH HERE, I GUESS.>
<ACTUALLY... THE LANDLADY SAYS WE NEED TO BE OUT OF HERE BY MIDNIGHT OR I GET TOSSED IN THE TRASH.>
WOO HOO! I FOUND MY "COOL THING"!

‹SO, WHERE WE GOIN'?›

WOO, SHINY!

Conscience Enforcement Authority (CEA)
Special Counseling Division

FIELD REPORT
Client: Piro
Case Worker: Seraphim
Case: CEA-010844FGP21224-4S
Status: Level 6, no change

Comments:

While interesting, the Piro case is extremely frustrating. After several months, he remains stranded in Japan and is currently homeless. Surprisingly, he is currently employed.

Unfortunately, I believe that most of what he earns will be spent before he leaves the store.

The chances of him saving enough for plane tickets back to the US are slim.

I am concerned that Piro lacks the aggressiveness and positive attitude he will need to resolve his current situation. He is in way over his head. I am hopeful that additional counseling and 'encouragement' will help him conquer his current set of problems.

Footnote:

My 'assistant', Boo, has actually succeeded in making Largo worse than he was before. Due to the lack of professional support from the home office, I reserve the right to implement special tactics where and when I deem fit. Once again, I submit my futile request for additional funds, equipment and resources.

Seraphim - Conscience Operative, Level 9

[send document... done]

[close window]
[open recent documents]
[open **seraphim-resume.2002**]

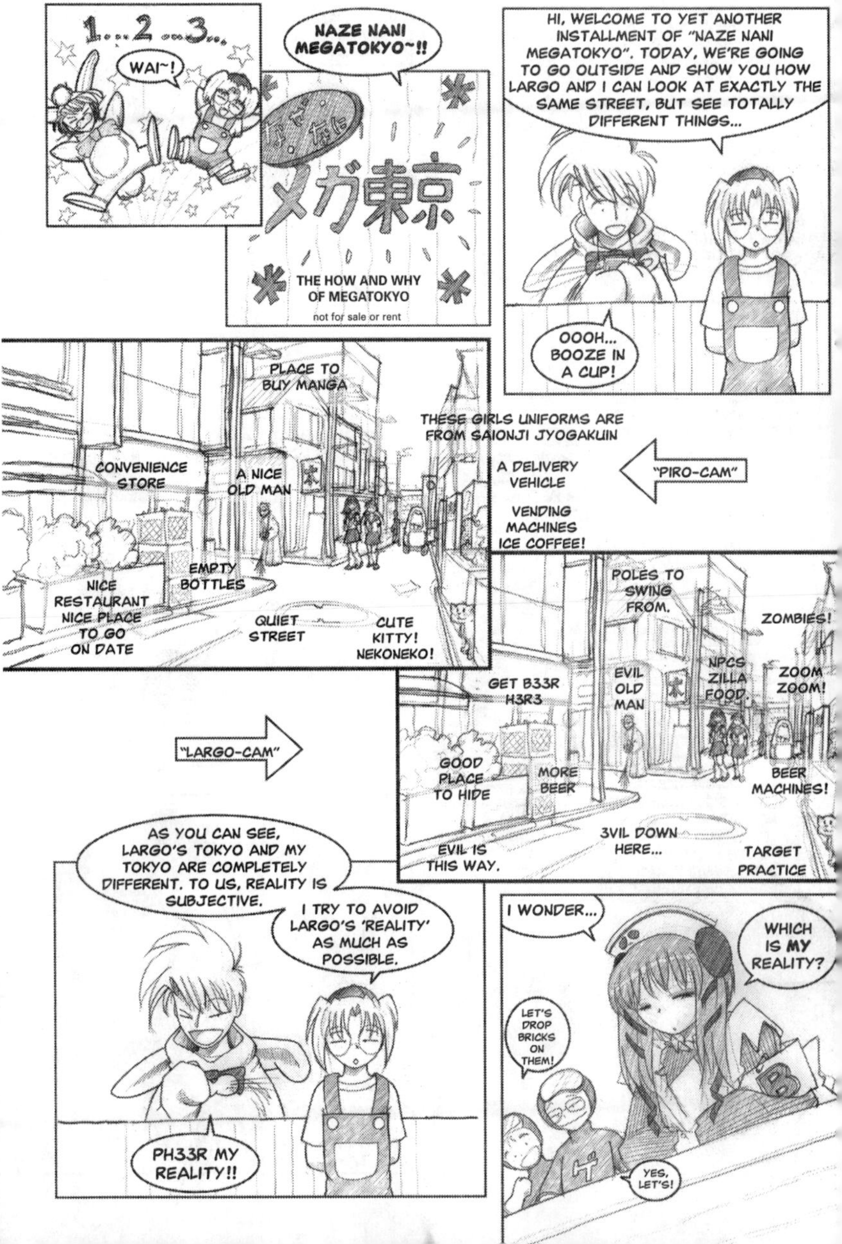
1...2...3...
WAI~!
NAZE NANI MEGATOKYO~!!
メガ東京
THE HOW AND WHY OF MEGATOKYO
not for sale or rent
HI, WELCOME TO YET ANOTHER INSTALLMENT OF "NAZE NANI MEGATOKYO". TODAY, WE'RE GOING TO GO OUTSIDE AND SHOW YOU HOW LARGO AND I CAN LOOK AT EXACTLY THE SAME STREET, BUT SEE TOTALLY DIFFERENT THINGS...
OOOH... BOOZE IN A CUP!
PLACE TO BUY MANGA
THESE GIRLS UNIFORMS ARE FROM SAIONJI JYOGAKUIN
CONVENIENCE STORE
A NICE OLD MAN
A DELIVERY VEHICLE
"PIRO-CAM"
VENDING MACHINES ICE COFFEE!
EMPTY BOTTLES
NICE RESTAURANT NICE PLACE TO GO ON DATE
QUIET STREET
CUTE KITTY! NEKONEKO!
POLES TO SWING FROM.
ZOMBIES!
GET B33R H3R3
EVIL OLD MAN
NPCS ZILLA FOOD.
ZOOM ZOOM!
"LARGO-CAM"
GOOD PLACE TO HIDE
MORE BEER
BEER MACHINES!
EVIL IS THIS WAY.
3VIL DOWN HERE...
TARGET PRACTICE
AS YOU CAN SEE, LARGO'S TOKYO AND MY TOKYO ARE COMPLETELY DIFFERENT. TO US, REALITY IS SUBJECTIVE.
I TRY TO AVOID LARGO'S 'REALITY' AS MUCH AS POSSIBLE.
PH33R MY REALITY!!
I WONDER...
WHICH IS MY REALITY?
LET'S DROP BRICKS ON THEM!
YES, LET'S!

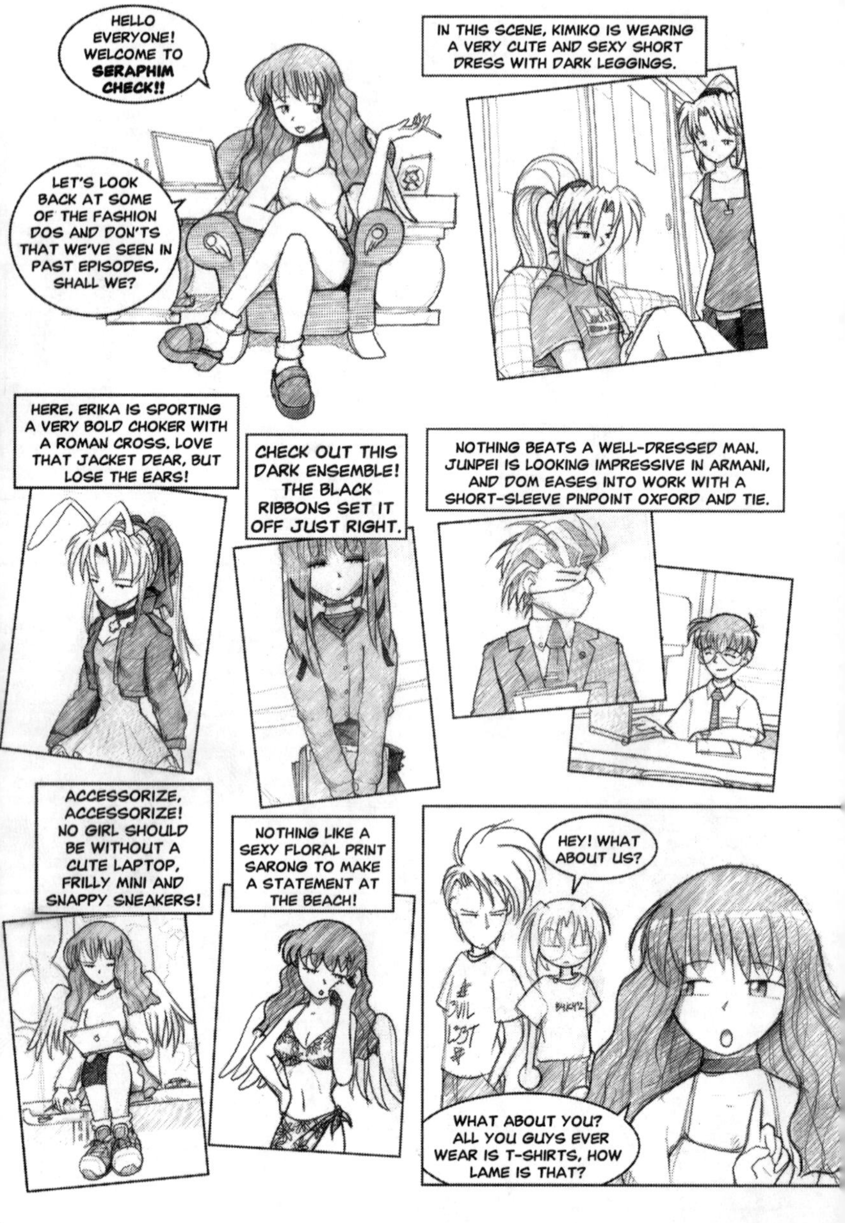
HELLO EVERYONE! WELCOME TO SERAPHIM CHECK!!
LET'S LOOK BACK AT SOME OF THE FASHION DOS AND DON'TS THAT WE'VE SEEN IN PAST EPISODES, SHALL WE?
IN THIS SCENE, KIMIKO IS WEARING A VERY CUTE AND SEXY SHORT DRESS WITH DARK LEGGINGS.
HERE, ERIKA IS SPORTING A VERY BOLD CHOKER WITH A ROMAN CROSS. LOVE THAT JACKET DEAR, BUT LOSE THE EARS!
CHECK OUT THIS DARK ENSEMBLE! THE BLACK RIBBONS SET IT OFF JUST RIGHT.
NOTHING BEATS A WELL-DRESSED MAN. JUNPEI IS LOOKING IMPRESSIVE IN ARMANI, AND DOM EASES INTO WORK WITH A SHORT-SLEEVE PINPOINT OXFORD AND TIE.
ACCESSORIZE, ACCESSORIZE! NO GIRL SHOULD BE WITHOUT A CUTE LAPTOP, FRILLY MINI AND SNAPPY SNEAKERS!
NOTHING LIKE A SEXY FLORAL PRINT SARONG TO MAKE A STATEMENT AT THE BEACH!
HEY! WHAT ABOUT US?
WHAT ABOUT YOU? ALL YOU GUYS EVER WEAR IS T-SHIRTS, HOW LAME IS THAT?

THE LAST COMIC YOU READ WAS TECHNICALLY THE END OF CHAPTER 0.

WE DID A LOT OF COMICS THAT WERE NOT REALLY PART OF THE STORY BUT WERE MORE LIKE 'ONE SHOT' STAND ALONE EPISODES. MANY OF THESE STAND QUITE WELL ON THEIR OWN, SO I'VE PULLED THEM OUT AND GROUPED THEM TOGETHER HERE AT THE END OF THE BOOK TO GIVE THE STORY BETTER FLOW.

LARGO PUT THIS ONE TOGETHER USING FRAMES FROM PREVIOUS COMICS. UNFORTUNATELY, I'VE LOST THE ORIGINAL ART FOR FRAME 1, SO WHAT YOU SEE HERE IS A 'WEB RESOLUTION' VERSION.

OUT OF EVERYTHING IN CHAPTER 0, I LOST ONLY TWO PIECES OF ART. NOT BAD, CONSIDERING.

REMEMBER WHEN THE PLAYSTATION 2 CAME OUT?

THIS IS A "BAD ART DAY SPECIAL" BECAUSE I DIDN'T TRACE AND CLEAN THE IMAGES BEFORE PUTTING THE COMIC TOGETHER. EVEN SO, IT DIDN'T COME OUT TOO BAD.

LARGO LOVES TO POKE FUN AT PEOPLE IN THE GAMING INDUSTRY.
HE REALLY WANTED TO GET US INTO TROUBLE, I THINK.

THE IDEA OF WIGGLING AROUND A CARDBOARD CUTOUT REALLY CRACKED ME UP FOR SOME REASON. ROMERO IS SO MUCH FUN TO DRAW.

WE OWE A LOT OF OUR SUCCESS WITH MEGATOKYO TO THE GENEROUS LINKAGE FROM A VERY POPULAR WEBCOMIC CALLED "PENNY ARCADE".

PENNY ARCADE USED HAVE A SITE WHERE YOU COULD MAKE YOUR OWN PENNY ARCADE COMIC CALLED 'THE BENCH'. THIS WAS OUR SUBMISSION.

OH, IT SAYS "FAN APPRECIATION BAT", ON THE BAT. I'VE OFTEN FELT THAT I NEED ONE OF THOSE.

NEEDLESS TO SAY, LARGO'S ANTICIPATION OF THE NEW BIOWARE GAME "NEVERWINTER NIGHTS" BORDERED ON THE CLINICALLY OBSESSIVE.

THANK GOD THE GUYS AT BIOWARE HAVE SUCH A GREAT SENSE OF HUMOR. CANADIANS ARE COOL.

LARGO WANTED TO DO A LOT OF THESE "PSA" OR "PUBLIC SERVICE ANNOUNCEMENT" TYPE STRIPS.

I SWEAR, I'LL NEVER UNDERSTAND THIS WHOLE "ZOMBIE" THING.

WE GOT A LOT OF EMAIL FROM "RAVERS" WHO WERE OFFENDED BY THIS COMIC - AND AT THE SAME TIME GOT EMAIL FROM RAVERS WHO THOUGHT IT WAS A HOOT.

FOR THE RECORD, I LOVE RAVE CULTURE. I'M A BIG MUSIC FAN - I LISTEN TO EVERYTHING FROM TRANCE, TECHNO, EBM, HOUSE AND INDUSTRIAL TO DOWNTEMPO, AMBIENT AND CHILL. INTERNET RADIO ROCKS.

I'VE MOVED TWICE TIMES SINCE I STARTED MEGATOKYO. I HATE MOVING.

YES, THIS REALLY DID HAPPEN. THANK GOD WE EMPTIED THE DRAWERS FIRST.

SPECIAL! ANIME CENTRAL 2001 SNAPSHOT

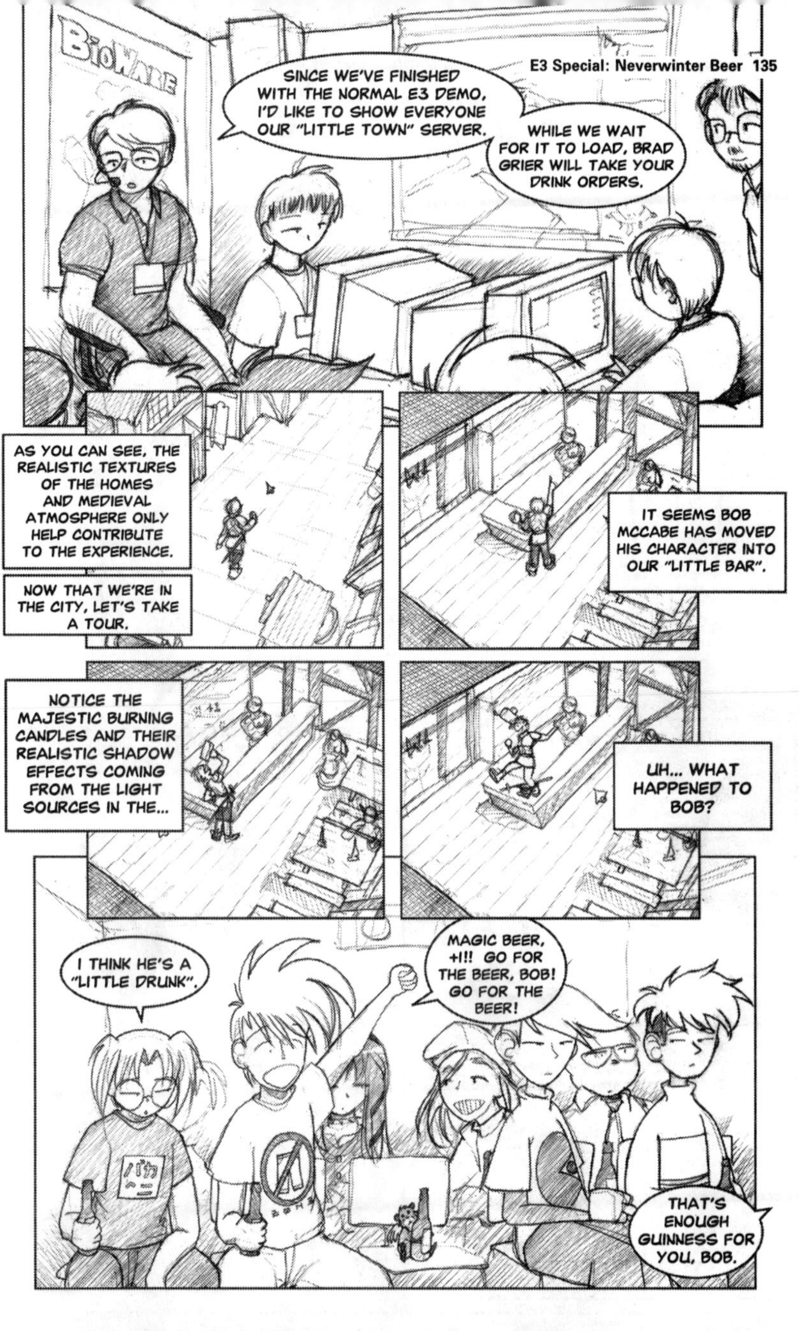
SINCE WE'VE FINISHED WITH THE NORMAL E3 DEMO, I'D LIKE TO SHOW EVERYONE OUR "LITTLE TOWN" SERVER.
WHILE WE WAIT FOR IT TO LOAD, BRAD GRIER WILL TAKE YOUR DRINK ORDERS.
AS YOU CAN SEE, THE REALISTIC TEXTURES OF THE HOMES AND MEDIEVAL ATMOSPHERE ONLY HELP CONTRIBUTE TO THE EXPERIENCE.
NOW THAT WE'RE IN THE CITY, LET'S TAKE A TOUR.
IT SEEMS BOB MCCABE HAS MOVED HIS CHARACTER INTO OUR "LITTLE BAR".
NOTICE THE MAJESTIC BURNING CANDLES AND THEIR REALISTIC SHADOW EFFECTS COMING FROM THE LIGHT SOURCES IN THE...
UH... WHAT HAPPENED TO BOB?
I THINK HE'S A "LITTLE DRUNK".
MAGIC BEER, +1!! GO FOR THE BEER, BOB! GO FOR THE BEER!
THAT'S ENOUGH GUINNESS FOR YOU, BOB.

SERAPHIM ART-DAY SPECIAL!

SINCE PIRO IS GOOFING OFF AT E3 THIS WEEKEND, I'LL BE HANGING WITH MY CO-WORKER AND GIRLFRIEND, EM.

HI!

FIRST OFF, THE PS-7000 OVERHEAD SCANNER AT WORK NEEDS SOME 'ADJUSTMENTS'.

THINK "OFFICE SPACE".

THEN, WE DONNED OUR 'PERIL SENSITIVE SUNGLASSES' IN TRIBUTE TO THE PASSING OF DOUGLAS ADAMS.

IT'S ONLY SCARY IF YOU SEE IT COMMIN'.

PIRO'S AMEX CARD HAS NO PRESET SPENDING LIMITS. I ASSUMED THAT HE WOULDN'T NEED IT IN LA.

WANNA HIT EVERY STORE IN THE MALL?

SURE! PIRO WOULD NEVER SUGGEST THAT!

PIRO, I HOPE YOU ARE ENJOYING YOUR STAY IN LA. IF YOU NEED A FEW MORE DAYS, I THINK WE'LL MANAGE.

SO, WHAT DO WE DO NEXT TIME PIRO LEAVES TOWN?

I'M THINKING 'EUROPE'.

TWO AND A HALF HOURS OF ESCAPISM...

I HOPE PIRO DIDN'T WANT TO SEE "THE MUMMY RETURNS".

NAH, IT'S NOT ANIMATED AND IT'S IN ENGLISH.

dead piro day

YEA, QUITE DEAD, REALLY. I'M SORRY FOLKS - I NEED TO SKIP ON TODAY'S COMIC.
PLEASE DON'T SHOOT ME. I'VE GOT A BAD COLD AND I NEED TO CATCH UP ON SLEEP.
IT WAS A HARD WEEK AT WORK. :)

I'VE GOT SOMETHIN' SPECIAL PLANNED OVER THE WEEKEND, I JUST
NEED A WEE BIT OF TIME TO REST FIRST. IT'LL MAKE YOU CHUCKLE.
THANKS EVERYONE!

AROUND THE TIME OF THE "ANNA MILLER'S" COMIC I HAD A PRETTY BAD COLD. TIRED, GRUMPY, AND NOT WANTING TO DRAW ANYTHING, I DID THIS "DEAD PIRO DAY" JOKE. FOR SOME REASON, THE TERM "DEAD PIRO DAY" STUCK.

WHENEVER I CAN'T MANAGE TO GET A COMIC DONE, I EITHER RESORT TO HAVING DOM TOURTURE PEOPLE WITH STICK FIGURE COMICS, OR I DO A SINGLE "DEAD PIRO DAY" DRAWING AND POST THAT. SOME DPD'S ACTUALLY CAME OUT PRETTY NICE.

FOR A WHILE I EXPERIMENTED WITH JUST DRAWING THE FIRST FRAME OF THE NEXT COMIC AND POSTING THAT AS A KIND OF PREVIEW.

IT WAS KIND OF NICE BECAUSE YOU COULD SEE A LITTLE MORE DETAIL THAN YOU WOULD IN A NORMAL SIZE FRAME AT WEB RESOLUTION.

dead piro preview day

(SORRY FOLKS, NO COMIC TODAY. HERE'S A PREVIEW OF MONDAY'S COMIC. I NEED THE WEEKEND TO RE-GROUP AND GET SOME (GASP) SLEEP. TUNE IN MONDAY AS WE FINALLY GET BACK ON TRACK WITH THE COMIC AND THE RANTS. THANKS FOR THE SUPPORT! –PIRO.)

<WHAT AM I DOING?>

BUT IN THE END I DECIDED THAT IT WAS MORE OF A COP-OUT THAN SOMETHING THAT WAS REALLY ENTERTAINING.

MT FANS HAVE BEEN VERY PATIENT. THERE HAVE BEEN A LOT OF DELAYS AND MISSED COMICS OVER THE PAST TWO YEARS, AND I'VE FELT BAD ABOUT EVERY SINGLE ONE.

I GUESS THAT'S WHY I TRIED SO MANY DIFFERENT IDEAS ABOUT WHAT I COULD POST WHEN A NORMAL COMIC WASN'T POSSIBLE.

(YES THAT
IS A 'PIRO'
KEYCHAIN :)

PIRO ART DAY SPECIAL #001

KIMIKO NANASAWA

M E G A + o k y o

THE "PIRO ART DAY
SPECIAL" OF KIMIKO
ON THE PREVIOUS
PAGE HAS ALWAYS
BUGGED ME
BECAUSE THE
PROPORTIONS ARE
WAY OUT OF WACK.

I'VE TAKEN SOME
TIME TO RE-DRAW
THIS IMAGE THE WAY
IT SHOULD LOOK.

OH, AND IF YOU ARE
THE PERSON WHO
BOUGHT THE
ORIGINAL DRAWING
OF THIS AT ANIME
CENTRAL - PLEASE
LET YOU KNOW, I'LL
SEND YOU THIS
REVISED VERSION TO
REPLACE IT.

KIMIKO NANASAWA
MEGATOKYO

F 11
08
02
FRED GALLAGHER

I HOPE YOU'VE ENJOYED READING MEGATOKYO, VOLUME I. IT'S BEEN FUN GOING BACK TO THE BEGINNING AND VISITING HOW IT ALL STARTED.

IF YOU ARE ALREADY A MEGATOKYO READER AND HAVE BEEN READING IT ONLINE, I WANT TO SAY A BIG "THANK YOU" FOR YOUR SUPPORT. WHEN LARGO AND I STARTED THIS, WE NEVER IMAGINED THAT IT WOULD HAVE GAINED THE POPULARITY IT SEEMS TO HAVE TODAY. WITHOUT YOUR FAITHFUL SUPPORT AND INFINITE PATIENCE, MEGATOKYO WOULD BE JUST A FEW RANDOM COMICS SITTING ON MY HARD DRIVE.

IF THIS IS YOUR FIRST TIME READING MEGATOKYO, I HOPE THAT YOU'VE ENJOYED IT. IF YOU DID, YOU CAN CONTINUE READING THE STORY BY VISITING THE WEBSITE ITSELF – **WWW.MEGATOKYO.COM**. NOT ONLY WILL YOU BE ABLE TO PICK UP WHERE THIS BOOK LEAVES OFF, BUT YOU CAN READ A BRAND NEW COMIC EVERY MONDAY, WEDNESDAY AND FRIDAY. YES, THE STORY IS STILL PLODDING ALONG.

SO, FROM EVERYONE HERE INVOLVED WITH MEGATOKYO, THANK YOU FOR READING, AND SEE YOU ONLINE!

DON'T TELL THEM THAT! MAKE THEM BUY THE NEXT VOLUME! BAKA!!!

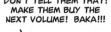

(OUR PUBLISHER KEI)

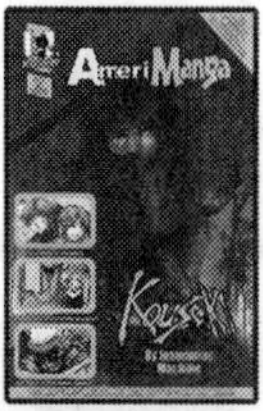
AmeriManga

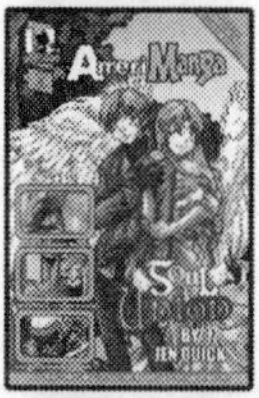
AmeriManga

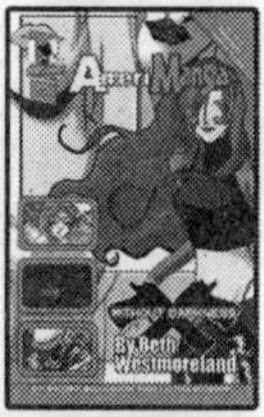
By Beth Westmoreland

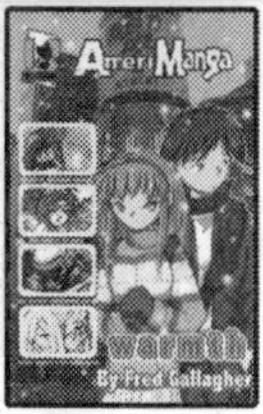
AmeriManga
warmth
By Fred Gallagher

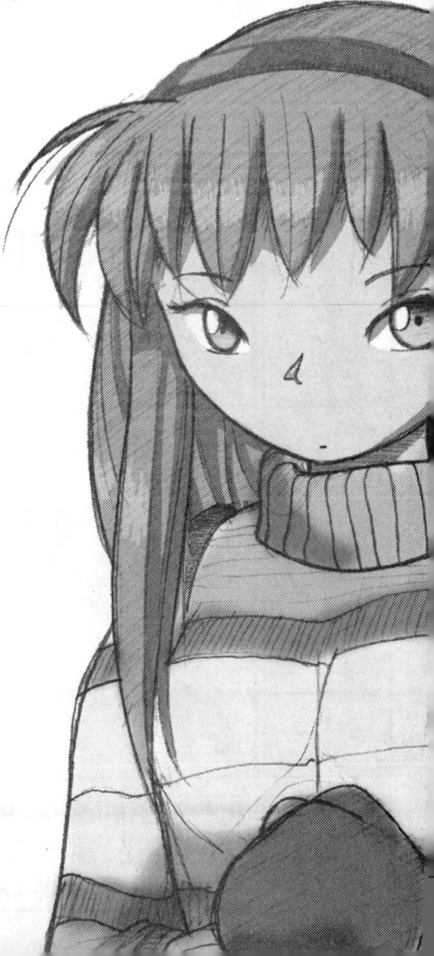

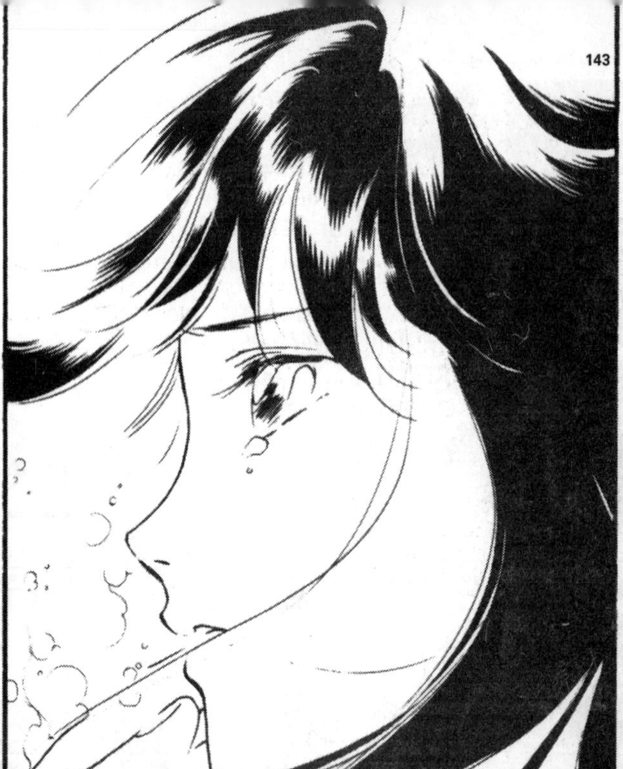

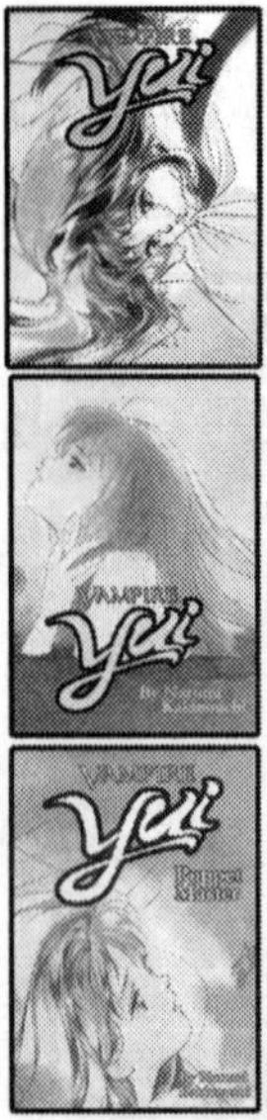
VAMPIRE
Yui

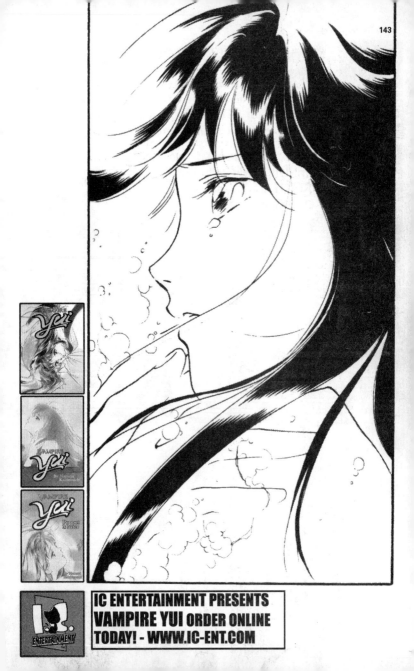